ATRA

An Ancient Hebrew Deluge Story and Other Flood Story Fragments

By

Albert T. Clay

THE BOOK TREE
San Diego, California

First published 1922
Yale University Press
New Haven, CT

ISBN 1-58509-228-2

Cover layout & design
Lee Berube

Printed on Acid-Free Paper
in the United States of America

Published by
The Book Tree
P O Box 16476
San Diego, CA 92176
www.thebooktree.com

INTRODUCTION

The word Atrahasis means "extra wise" and is the name for the earliest known version of Noah, or Ut-napishtim, who built an ark and saved mankind from destruction. This is that story, which many scholars believe was the original from which all known flood stories came from. For over five thousand years this story has survived and was translated into many languages throughout the ancient world.

Atrahasis was the most popular story in the ancient world, telling how he and his wife survived the flood and how he was granted a form of immortality by the gods. This is also a fascinating story of the gods and how they were involved with the flood. We find in this tale the very first mention of the ancient Mesopotamian gods and goddesses—Anu, Enlil, Ea, (or Enki), Marduk, Inanna, Ninurta and Mami (the mother goddess), among others. Collectively, they were referred to as the Anunnaki.

This story reveals that the Anunnaki was in complete control of the earth—of that there is no doubt. They were tired of the noise and overpopulation of the planet, so created the flood to eliminate humanity. Enki, however, sided with mankind and did not wish them to perish. Atrahasis had a special connection to his god, Enki—they would speak back and forth. With Enki's help, he was able to prepare for the flood and survive.

We discover from this story that it was not God himself who helped Atrahasis, as the story of Noah later relates, but one lone God out of many. In fact, he is the only one who cared enough about mankind to help them survive. The flood story was later changed to reflect one God in our monotheistic societies.

It is also clear that the flood was not a naturally occurring catastrophe, but specifically engineered or designed by the gods to rid them of a problem. Us. Only by the grace of one of them were we allowed to continue.

It seems that every culture worldwide has the mythological story of a flood—even in remote areas that have a history of isolation. It is the one story that we all seem to share. Why? And why do we not explore the oldest known version of the story carefully for clues? That is the purpose of this book.

Some scholars have been unafraid to question who these gods were. Despite the fact that these beings are clearly "gods" under any translation, which the contributor and translator of this book, Clay, reinforces, some have still declared them to be kings and rulers in order to avoid ridicule. They were gods. The *Atrahasis* constitutes one of the earliest forms of mythology, where we find the gods and goddesses in their usual positions of power and authority.

If we can someday prove that a worldwide flood took place, as opposed to occurring in isolated areas, it would go far in supporting the reality of the *Atrahasis* myth. Zecharia Sitchin has written a number of fascinating books on this subject, being one of less than 200 people in the world who can understand and translate the original cuneiform writings. He has presented interesting evidence from the fields of science, linguistics and archaeology in support of the reality of the gods and their purpose in coming to earth. Among many cuneiform texts, Sitchin used, as a primary source, the *Atrahasis*. A number of respected academic researchers have openly come to his support, while others have remained critical.

Until now, this story has been rather hard to find. Making it easily available allows the average person to read the tale, along with other material, and judge it for themselves. Were the gods human-like beings who came from elsewhere, having technology and powers beyond the scope of humans at the time, as this story seems to infer? Or were they figments of active imaginations, invented to tell a meaningful, mythological tale? It is hard to know because it first appeared in the remote past. Nevertheless, the *Atrahasis* is a great book for those interested in early mythology.

A number of other interesting flood story fragments round out this fascinating book.

Paul Tice

To my Colleague and Friend

PROFESSOR CHARLES CUTLER TORREY

FOREWORD

The title of this little monograph tells its own story, namely, that an ancient Hebrew deluge tradition written in cuneiform is here presented. It is not a recent discovery, nor is it the first time that it has appeared in print. It was first published a number of years ago, but owing to a faulty copy of the text originally presented, its importance has never been understood.

This story of the deluge which had found its way into Babylonia, where it was made to conform largely to the Akkadian dialect, fully betrays its origin; it came from the same source whence the Hebrew traditions came, namely from the people who lived in Amurru (Syria and Mesopotamia), called the Amorites. As was the case in pre-Mosaic days, and to a large extent in early Israel, when henotheism prevailed, "God" is the foremost deity. We learn from this tradition, and also from its redaction written centuries later, that a long famine preceded the deluge, which is not referred to in the Old Testament, that the famine had been sent because men had multiplied, and also because of their clamor, reminding us of the causes given for the deluge in the Old Testament.

The great importance of this inscription, which was copied about the time of Abraham from an older tablet, together with other facts here presented, is that it will require that the prevailing view be abandoned that the Hebrew traditions were borrowed from Babylonia. This involves many scholarly works written in recent decades upon the early history of Israel. It has been generally held that these stories are of Babylonian origin; that Canaan was a domain of Babylonian culture in the time of Moses; and that Israel had assimilated this foreign culture as well as its religion, "feathers and all." Not only is the Israelitish cult held to be dependent upon the Babylonian, but also many of the chief characters are said to have descended from Babylonian mythology. In Germany where these views developed, some scholars have gone to great extremes; only a change of names had taken place, and Marduk or Bel was transformed into Christ. In America a more moderate position has generally been accepted, in which the extreme views were toned down, and the Pan-Babylonian theory made more palatable. Nevertheless, it is generally held that these traditions had been brought from Babylonia in the time of Abraham, or in the Amarna Period, or at the time of the exile; and that many of the characters had their origin in myth.

Twelve years ago the writer took issue with this general position, holding that the traditions of the Hebrews were indigenous in the land of the Amorites; and that contrary to the prevailing view, this land was not dependent for its population upon Arabs who migrated from Arabia a little before and after the time of Abraham, but upon an indigenous people, the antiquity of whose culture is as high as that known in Egypt or Babylonia; and also that the Semites who moved into the lower Euphrates valley mainly came from this quarter, and brought with them their culture. He has also consistently maintained that such familiar Biblical characters as the patriarchs and others, instead of being the creations of fiction writers, were historical personages.

While the new point of view was accepted by many scholars, and the tremendous flow of Pan-Babylonian literature was suddenly and very materially reduced in volume, only a few of those who had written upon the subject acknowledged the gains that had been made, and reversed their positions. Even some scholars in their efforts to nullify the advances, instead of facing the real issue in their reviews, dwelt upon and held up as proof of the writer's thesis some extraneous suggestions which had been intended for consideration in filling in the background of the two or more millenniums of Amorite history prior to Abraham.

The writer's thesis in brief is, that the Arabian origin of the Semites living in ancient Syria and Babylonia, including the Hebrews, is baseless; but that the antiquity of the Amorite civilization is very great; and also the assertion that the culture and religion of Israel were borrowed from Babylonia is without any foundation; for they were indigenous; and that the Semites who migrated to Babylonia with their culture were mainly from Amurru. In the judgment of the writer the material presented in this little monograph, as well as in his recently published *Empire of the Amorites,* will require a very extensive readjustment of many views bearing upon the subject, as well as the abandonment of many others. Moreover, it also has bearings of a far-reaching character on many other Old Testament problems.

Amurru, called "the land of the Amorites," it might be added, is a geographical term which was used in ancient times for the great stretch of territory between Babylonia and the Mediterranean. By reason of its products and its position this land had been attractive to other peoples ever since one strove to obtain what the other possessed, resulting in almost innumerable invasions and conflicts taking place in this land. Within the historical period we know that the Babylonians, Egyptians, Hittites, Assyrians, Persians, Greeks, Romans, Arabs, Turks, and other peoples controlled this territory. It should be added that this country in turn also prevailed at times over other lands, notably Babylonia and Egypt. In these pages we have evidence that one of its rulers conquered Babylonia as early as 4000 B.C.

This country has always represented ethnologically a great mixture. Linguistically, as far as is known, a Semitic language has always prevailed in this great stretch of territory. The Amorite or Hebrew language, being the oldest of which we have knowledge, was followed by the Aramaic, and later by the Arabic which now prevails. To what extent the Akkadian dialect was used in certain parts, and what script was employed in the early period, are as yet undetermined. Excavations at one or two well selected sites will throw light on this and many other questions, and furnish us with the material whereby we will be able to reconstruct many chapters of its early history.

It gives the writer great pleasure to inscribe this little contribution to his colleague and friend, Professor Charles Cutler Torrey, who not only has watched sympathetically these investigations advance, but also in reading the manuscript has made a number of suggestions as well as several identifications of roots which are indicated in the foot notes.

ALBERT T. CLAY.

NEW HAVEN, CONN.,
May 19, 1922.

CONTENTS

APPENDIX

I

AN ANCIENT HEBREW DELUGE STORY

This fragment of a large tablet was published in text, transliteration and translation nearly twenty-five years ago, before it had come into the possession of the Pierpont Morgan Library Collection of Babylonian Inscriptions; in the meantime many other translations have appeared.[1] Moreover, owing to the form in which the tablet had been presented, due somewhat to its not having been thoroughly cleaned, its importance has only been slightly appreciated. While it was understood that it had the same general application as a legend preserved in the British Museum, known as the Ea and Atra-ḫasis legend, and belonging to a later period, the latter, owing to its fragmentary condition, could not be said to refer to the deluge. Moreover, while it was apparent that the present text did refer to the deluge, it was considered even by one who examined the tablet that it "contained little more than a few phrases and words, without any coherent connection."[2] Further study, however, as will be seen from what follows, reveals the fact that this is a mistake; that it is a part of an old version of what should properly be called the Atra-ḫasis Epic, which is a very ancient Hebrew or Amorite Deluge Story; and that the so-called Ea and Atra-ḫasis Legend of the Assyrian period, which has also been translated by a number of scholars,[3] is a late redaction of it. The later version or redaction was put into a magical setting for incantation purposes. In the Appendix will be found the transliteration and translation of all the versions of this deluge story or stories, both cuneiform and Greek. The ancient dated text is designated as A, and the late redaction as B.

[1] Scheil *Recueil de Travaux* 20 (1898) 55 ff; Jensen *KB* VI 1 288 ff; Dhorme *Choix de Textes Religieux Assyro-Babyloniens* 120 ff; Ungnad *Altorientalische Texte und Bilder* I, 57 f; Rogers *Cuneiform Parallels* 104 ff; etc.

[2] Hilprecht *BE* Ser. D, V 1 p. 44.

[3] *CT* 15, 49. Translated by Zimmern *ZA* 14, 277 ff; Jensen *KB* VI 1 274 ff; Dhorme *Ibidem* 128 ff; Ungnad *ATB* I 61 ff; Rogers *Cuneiform Parallels* 113 ff and others.

A small fragment in the British Museum, ostensibly from a version of the Atra-ḫasis Epic, for it mentions the hero's name, which was also written in the late period, furnishes us with the conversation between the god Ea and Atra-ḫasis concerning the construction of the ship, and with what it should be loaded.[4] This is designated in the Appendix as C.

A few years ago there was published a brief epitomized history of the world, written in Sumerian, beginning with the creation, followed by an account of the building of cities and the story of the deluge. This tablet was found during the excavations at Nippur conducted by the University of Pennsylvania. The tablet was written after the Sumerian language had ceased to be spoken in its purity, some time between the middle of the First Dynasty of Babylon and the second Nîsin era, that is between 2300 and 1300 B. C.[5] Like the other legend written in the late period, it seems to have been used for incantation purposes. It is evidently based upon the same story as that from which the Gilgamesh Epic story has descended, as is apparent from several expressions found in it. The phrase in the Sumerian version "when for seven days and nights the flood overwhelms the land" (D, V: 3, 4) is paralleled in the Semitic by "six days and nights the wind drives; the deluge-tempest overwhelms the land, when the seventh day arrives, the tempest subsides in the onslaught" (E, 128-130). The reference also to "the wall," when the hero was apprised of the impending deluge, is in both. Further, the title of the hero, Um-napishtim, is replaced in the Sumerian by Zi-û-suddu, which is composed of three elements, Zi (*napishtim*) "life," and û (*ûm*) "day," to which the element suddu (*rêqu*) "to be distant" has been added. It is not impossible that Um-napishtim, which contains two of the three elements of the Sumerian name, is an abbreviated form of the original (see below). This version is designated as D.

The hero of the other and well known deluge story, which in the late period had been woven into the Gilgamesh Epic, is Atra-ḫasis,

[4] Delitzsch *Assyr. Les.*[3] p. 101; *KB* VI 1 254 ff; etc.

[5] See Poebel *Historical and Grammatical Texts* No. 1; and *Historical Texts* 14 ff; and 66 ff.

but his title, which is better known in connection with the story, is Um-napishtim, or Uta-napishtim.[6] This is designated as E.

Besides these versions or fragments of versions there is also known a little fragment of thirteen partially preserved lines, written probably in the Cassite period (about 1400 B.C.), in which neither the name of a god nor that of the hero is preserved.[7] This is designated as F.

The deluge story handed down by Berossus, in which the hero is Xisuthros (Σισουθρος), which name represents a transposition of the elements of Atra-ḫasis, i. e., Ḫasis-atra, is still another version of the epic.[8] This is designated as G.

The only dated version written in cuneiform is the one in the Pierpont Morgan Collection. It was copied from a still earlier inscription by a junior scribe named Azag-Aya, on the 28th day of Shebet, in the 11th year of Ammi-zaduga (1966 B.C.), which date is about 1300 years earlier than the time of the Library of Ashurbanipal (668-626 B.C.), to which the late redaction of it, now in the British Museum, belonged. The original from which the scribe copied had already been injured in the 12th line, which is indicated by the word *ḫibiš* "broken." How much earlier the previous text was written, cannot be surmised; but there are reasons for believing it is a very ancient legend, probably written two thousand years earlier (see below).

Unfortunately, the tablet has been injured since it was first published twenty-five years ago. Several small pieces have been lost from the surface of it. In the copy of the inscription, given in the Appendix, these parts are based upon the original copy made twenty-five years ago, and are indicated by small ink dots, easily recognized.

[6] See Haupt *Nimrod-Epos* 134 ff; Delitzsch *Ass. Les.*[3] 99 ff; *KB* VI 1 228 ff; Dhorme *Textes Religieux Assyro-Babyloniens* 100 ff; Ungnad *ATB* I, 50 ff. Rogers *Cuneiform Parallels* 90 ff.

[7] Hilprecht *BE* Ser. D V 1 p. 48. This fragment, if it actually came from Nippur, belongs to the Cassite period. This conclusion is based on a palaeographical and linguistic study of texts found at Nippur belonging to the Ḫammurabi and the Cassite periods. If the text came from Sippar, which is more likely, or from some other Semitic city, then it is possible that it was written at a somewhat earlier time.

[8] See Zimmern *KAT*[3] 543 f.

The fragment shows that the tablet, of which it was a part, had eight columns. This can be determined from the shape of the fragment, the second column of which, not being complete, does not reach the thickest part of the tablet, i.e., the middle. It can also be determined that it had eight columns from the number of lines.[9] Deducting those of the last column, namely 37, from the total number of the tablet, which is 439, leaves 402; which divided into the remaining seven columns, gives 57 or 58 for each. This can be verified by adding 37 to the nearly 20 preserved in the seventh column, which equals 57.

This fragment of the ancient version contains the opening lines of what was the second tablet of the series, which was entitled or known by the words *I-nu-ma i-lu a-we-lum.* This is an incomplete sentence meaning "When God, man," etc.[10] It recalls the well known title *Enuma Anu Enlil* "When Anu, Enlil," the complete form of which is known: "When Anu, Enlil, and Ea, the great gods, entrusted the great laws of heaven," etc. *Inuma ilu awêlum* were doubtless the initial words of the first tablet of the series.

What the content of the first tablet was cannot be surmised. Like the Sumerian text found at Nippur, and the first chapter of Genesis, it may have contained an account of the creation. This second tablet of the ancient version opens with a reference to the famine, as in the late redaction. In the latter we learn that the famine lasted six, probably seven years; and that it became so severe that human flesh was eaten. The Biblical story makes no reference to a famine preceding the deluge; nor does the Gilgamesh Epic story; yet in the light of the Atra-ḫasis Epic this would seem to be implied in the Gilgamesh story in the message which Ea tells Um-napishtim to give to the people, namely, "it will rain for you abundance," after the ship is built.

The famine in the ancient Atra-ḫasis version came after men began to multiply, and the land had become satiated "like a bull." This fact is hinted at in the late redaction where we have the line "[The people] have not become less; they are more numerous than before" (B, III: 39). It was ordered that the fig tree be cut off,

[9] This was determined when the tablet was originally published; see Scheil *RT* 20 55 ff.

[10] This was originally incorrectly read *i-nu-ma ṣal-lu a-we-lum* (see below).

that Adad withhold the rain; that the rivers be restrained at their source; that the fields withhold their produce; and that the womb be closed. The lines of the seventh column refer to the intervention of the god Ea, after Adad had opened the heavens and sent a deluge. The promise to preserve the seed of life is also referred to, as well as the entering into the ship.

What is preserved of the redactor's work makes no reference to the flood. Whether the redactor included in his work also the account of the deluge, the main theme of the epic, can be determined only when other parts of his incantation are found. The ancient version, however, enables us to ascertain where he obtained his account of the famine, which he used for incantation purposes, in connection with sickness and the bearing of children. The story of the famine involving the lack of fertility lent itself to such a purpose. That he modified, enlarged, and glossed it, is perfectly clear from the transliteration and translation of the two texts, the ancient and the redaction.

Complete translations of all the cuneiform deluge stories are given in the Appendix; but in order to have the related parts of the two texts of the Atra-ḫasis Epic together for the purpose of comparison, the following selections are here given: A, I: 1 to 19 of the former, and B, III: 2 to 8 and 37 to 59 of the latter.

Selection from the Early Version Lines 1-19.

[*li*]-(?)-*bi-il* [*ri*]-*ig*-[*ma-ši-i*]*n bal-ṭi-a*(?)	I will bring (?) their clamor (?) ......
ma-tum ir-ta-bi-iš ni-[*šu im*]-*ti-da*	The land had become great; the people had multiplied.
[*m*]*a-tum ki-ma li-i i-ša-ab-bu*	The land like a bull had become satiated.
[*i-na*] *ḫu-bu-ri-ši-na i-lu it-ta-aḫ-da-ar*	[In] their assemblage God was absent.
[......] *iš-te-me ri-gi-im-ši-in*	...... heard their clamor.
[*iz*]-*za-kar a-na el*(?)-*li ra-bu-tim*	He said to the great gods (?)
iq-ta-ab-ta ri-gi-im a-wi-lu-ti	Those observing the clamor of men.
i-na ḫu-bu-ri-ši-na iz-za-kar ma-ši-it-ta	In their assemblage he spoke of desolations.

[lip-par]-sa a-na ni-ši te-i-na	Let the fig tree for the people be [cut off].
[i-na ša-da]-ti-ši-na li-'-zu ša-am-mu	[In] their [fields], let the plant become a weed (?).
.... *šu ^{d}Adad li-ša-aq-ṭi-il*	...... the sheep let Adad destroy.
ḫi-bi-iš -a [li]-il-li-ka	[The fountains of the deep] let not flow.
[ia iš-ša-a me-li na]-aq-bi	[That the flood rise not at the so]urce.
[li-]-il-li-ik ša-ru	Let the wind blow.
[na]-ag-bi-ra li-e-ir-ri	Let it drive mightily.
[ur]-bi-e-tum li-im-ta-an-ni-ma	Let the clouds be held back, that
[zu-un-nu i-na šamê] (-e) ia it-tu-uk	[Rain from the heav]ens pour not forth.
[li-šu]-ur eqlu iš-bi-ki-šu	Let the field withhold its fertility.
[li-ni-'] ir-ta ša ^{d}Nisaba	[Let a change come over] the bosom of Nisaba.

Selections from the Redaction III 2-8, and 37-59.

[eli rig(ri-gi)-me-ši-na it-ta-d[ir]	[Concerning] their clamor he became troubled.
[izzakar ina] ḫu-bu-ri-ši-na la i-ṣa-ba-ta [ni-ši-tu]	[He spoke in] their assemblage to those untouched [by the desolations].
[^{d}En-l]il il-ta-kan pu-ḫur-[šu]	[Enlil) held [his] assembly.
[iz-za]-ka-ra a-na ilâni^{meš} marê^{meš}-šú	[He sa]id to the gods his children,
[iq]-tab-ta-ma [r]i-gi-im a-me-lu-te	Those observing the clamor of men:
[eli r]ig(ri-g[i)]-me-[ši-n]a at-ta-a-(di-ir)dir	[Concerning] their clamor I am troubled.
[izzakar ina] ḫu-[bu]-ri-ši-na la i-ṣa-ba-ta ni-ši-tu	[He said in] their assemblage to those untouched by the desolations.
[En-lil] il-ta-kan pu-ḫur-šú: izakkara a-na ilâni^{meš} mare^{meš}-šú	[Enlil] held his assembly; he speaks to the gods his children.
...... *ra me-e-ta aš-ku-na-ši-na-ti*	...... I will put them to death.

[nišê] la im-im-ṭa-a a-na ša pa-na i-ta-at-ra	[The people] have not become less; they are more numerous than before.
[eli] rig-me-ši-na at-ta-a-dir	[Concerning] their clamor I am troubled.
[izzakar ina] ḫu-bu-ri-ši-na la i-ṣa-ta ni-ši-tu	[He said in] their assemblage to those untouched by the desolations:
[lip-par]-sa-ma a-na ni-še-e ti-ta	Let the fig tree for the people be [cut off.]
[i-n]a kar-ši-ši-na li-me-ṣu šam-mu	[I]n their bellies let the plant be wanting.
[e]liš ^{d}*Adad zu-un-na-šú lu-ša-qir*	Above, let Adad make his rain scarce.
[li-is]-sa-kir šap-liš ia iš-ša-a me-lu i-na na-aq-bi	Below let (the fountain of the deep) be stopped that the flood rise not at the source.
[l]i-šur eqlu iš-pi-ki-e-šú	Let the field withhold its fertility.
[l]i-ni-' irtu ša ^{d}*Nisaba : mušâ-ti*^{meš} *lip-ṣu-u ugârê*^{meš}	Let a change come over the bosom of Nisaba; by night let the fields become white.
ṣeru pal-ku-ú lu-li-id id-ra-nu	Let the wide field bear weeds (?).
[li]-bal-kat ki-ri-im-ša : šam-mu ia ú-ṣa-a šu-ú- ia i-'-ru	Let her bosom revolt, that the plant come not forth, that the sheep become not pregnant.
[li]š-ša-kin-ma a-na nisê^{meš} *a-sa-ku*	Let calamity be placed upon the people.
[rêmu] lu-ku-ṣur-ma ia ú-še-šir šir-ra	Let the [womb] be closed, that it bring forth no infant.
ip-[par-s]u a-na ni-še-e ti-ta	The fig tree was cut [off] for the people.
i-na kar-ši-ši-na e-me-ṣu šam-mu	In their bellies, the plant was wanting.
e-liš ^{d}*Adad zu-un-na-šú u-ša-qir*	Above, Adad made scarce his rain.
is-sa-kir šap-liš ul iš-ša-a me-lu ina na-aq-bi	Below (the fountain of the deep) was stopped, that the flood rose not at the source.
iš-šur eqlu iš-pi-ki-šu	The field withheld its fertility.
i-ni-' irtu ša ^{d}*Nisaba: mušâti*^{meš} *ip-ṣu-u ugârê*^{meš}	A change came over the bosom of Nisaba; the fields by night became white.

ṣeru pal-ku-ú ú-li-id id-ra-na: ib-bal-kat ki-ri-im-ša	The wide field bore weeds (?); her womb revolted.
šam-mu ul ú-ṣa-a šú-ú ul i'-ru	The plant came not forth; the sheep did not become pregnant.

The critical historical study of the late redactor's work is comparatively easy in this instance, because we have an original from which his work has descended. In the thirteen hundred years many copyists and redactors had doubtless taken part in transmitting the legend. How many times the text had been re-copied during the two or three thousand years of its history prior to the time the present early version was inscribed, cannot be surmised.

This old version contains absolutely nothing to suggest the idea that it had originally been written in Sumerian. On the contrary, it is clearly evident that it is of Amorite origin. Not only are the hero and the deities Amorite, but also certain words, which were not in current use in Akkadian.

One of the most striking Amorite words in the text is *ḫuburu* (line 4), which also is found in the redaction. This has been left untranslated in all the translations known to the writer except one, where the meaning "totalité" is given. The word unquestionably is West Semitic, and means "assemblage, association."[11] It is found also in the Creation Story, in *ummu ḫubur* "mother of the assembly (or association)"[12] of gods, the title of Tiâmat, "the mother of them all" (*muallidat gimrišun*), who was of West Semitic origin.[13] The redactor, fearing the word would not be understood by his Assyrian readers, inserted a line which follows in his transcription, reading "[En]-lil established his assembly"; in which he used the regular Assyrian word for "assembly" (*puḫru*).

The root of *it-ta-aḫ-da-ar* (A, 4) is not found in Akkadian, but it is in Hebrew, in *'adar* "to be absent, to be lacking;" in which

[11] See notes beneath the transliteration in the Appendix.

[12] King read it as a name *ummu ḫubur;* see *Seven Tablets of Creation,* p. 17. Zimmern translated *ḫubur* "Tiefe, Totenreich" *KAT*[3] 642 f; Jensen translated "Die Mutter des Nordens" *KB* VI 1, p. 7, and suggested other possibilities, as "ὠκεανός, Getöse, Sünde, Gesamtheit" pp. 308 and 541; Ungnad "Mutter Ḫubur" *ATB* I 9; and Ebeling "Die Mutter der Tiefe" *Altorientalische Texte und Untersuchungen* II 4, p. 22.

[13] See Clay *Amurru the Home of the Northern Semites* 49 f.

language the verbal forms occur also in the Niphal, see 2 Sam., 17: 26, Isaiah 40: 26, etc. Apparently the redactor did not understand the word, for he changed the sense, and wrote in his paraphrase "Concerning their clamor he was troubled" (*ittadir*) (B, III: 2).

The word *iq-ta-ab-ta* (A. 7) does not occur in Akkadian; it is Amorite. In Ethiopic and Aramaic, *'aqab* means " to observe, mark," etc. It is found in Hebrew with the meaning " to follow at the heel."

The word *ma-ši-it-ta* "desolations" (A, 8) is Hebrew; see Job 30: 3; Psalm 74: 3, etc. In the redaction, the word used is *ni-ši-tu*. This also is Hebrew (see Psalm 88: 13).

A very striking and important proof that the original story was Amorite or Hebrew is to be seen in the use of the word *te-i-na* (A, 9), which is the Hebrew word for "fig tree." This the early redactors had allowed to stand, but a later scribe, feeling that this would not be understood in his country where the fig was practically unknown, replaced the Hebrew word *te-i-na* with *ti-ta,* the Babylonian word for "fig tree." In Babylonian and Assyrian literature the word *tîtu* or *tîttu* is little more than known. In Hebrew literature, as in the present text, the word "fig tree" is synonymous with "prosperity." It was not in Babylonia nor in Assyria that man "dwelt under" and ate "every one of his fig tree," but in Syria (see Mic. 4: 4; Is. 36: 16, etc.).

Owing to the injury of the tablet it is not possible to say that *šu* (A, 11), translated "flock," is not the pronominal suffix, but the word *šu* which does occur in the redactor's paraphrase, is another Hebrew word meaning "flock, sheep," which is frequently found in the Old Testament.

In *li-ša-aq-ti-il* (A, 11) is to be seen an Amorite word which had not been used in Akkadian. Whether the redactor understood its meaning, we do not know; but he changed the wording; and he also condensed the six lines of the original which follow (A, 12 to 16) into one line (see B, II: 30 and III: 45). Not only do we find *lišaqtil* instead of *lušaqtil,* but note also *limtanni, lištarriq, lišaznin,* and perhaps also *lierri* and *imaššid.* This probably is a peculiarity of the early Amorite language in which the legend had been written.

In line 12 the word *ḫibiš* indicates that a previous tablet had been injured. The words [*i*]*a* [*li*]-*il-li-ka* "let not flow" are preserved at the end of the line. Probably the words *e-na-ta ta-ma-ta* "fountains of the deep," as in Genesis 7: 11, stood in the original, and an Akkadian scribe who lived in Babylonia, a land where springs are unknown, being in doubt as to the reading, wrote *ḫibiš,* "injured."

The root of *li-e-ir-ri* (A, 15) is doubtless to be found in Hebrew in the common *yarah* " to throw, hurl." This root was not in current use in Babylonia.

The root of *li-im-ta-an-ni-ma* (A, 16), is evidently the familiar Hebrew *mana'* "to withhold, to hold back," used in connection with rain, Amos 4: 7; of "showers," Jer. 3: 3, etc., but the root was not in current use in Babylonia.

If we had no other data to show that Nisaba (A, 19), the goddess of fertility, is Amorite, this passage would be sufficient; but we have. Naturally no one would question that Adad is the Amorite Hadad. And there can be no doubt, but that Ea also had his origin in the West.[15]

These words are all found in the first nineteen lines of the text. Naturally the words currently used in Babylonia, as well as in Amurru, are not discussed. It is to be noted that the hero, Atra-ḫasis, bears an Amorite name.[16] The fact that the determinative

[15] Scholars generally agree that Adad (*dIM*) and Nisaba are West Semitic. On Ea as an Amorite god, see Chiera *Lists of Personal Names* p. 39 f.; and Clay *Empire of the Amorites* p. 175.

[16] This name is generally considered to be two words meaning "exceedingly wise," "the very wise one." While the Babylonians used it as synonymous with these words, it was nevertheless a personal name, and this does not seem to have been its original meaning. Names compounded with Atar and Attar, also written Atra, Atram, with and without the determination, are numerous among West Semitic names, cf. *Atar-bi'di* (*-idri, -gabri, -ṣûri, -nûri, -ḫammu, -qamu,* etc.), see Tallqvist *APN* 252 and *NBN* 231. The Babylonians in making use of these West Semitic legends, having their own word *atru,* meaning "surplus," "abundant," made an etymological play upon the name, as was done so frequently in the O. T., interpreting it in their own legends as being synonymous with "very wise," as is done in the Etana and Adapu Epics. It will be noticed that in the Adapa fragment discussed below, the word *At-ra-ḫa-si-sa* is not written grammatically as two words in the sentence, but is looked upon as a name, synonymous with the idea "clever one." The same is true in the Etana Legend (*KB* VI 1 106: 39), where *A-tar-ḫa-si-sa* is in apposition with *ad-mu ṣi-iḫ-ru,* which is in the nominative case.

for man is placed before it, especially in this early period, makes it impossible to regard it here as being an epithet for a hero bearing another name.

These facts and others which follow, especially those in connection with the name *Ilu* "God" for the chief deity's name in this legend, prove conclusively that this was originally a Hebrew or Amorite Deluge Story.

If this is an Amorite legend we would expect to find also in the work of the late redactor or glossarist, Amorite words which had not been adopted by the Semitic Babylonians; and in this we are not disappointed. A comparison of the two texts shows how the redactor inserted glosses or parallel phrases in connection with *ḫuburišina, iqtabta,* etc., and as we already have seen, how he replaced the Hebrew *teina* with the Babylonian *tîtu,* and used the Hebrew word *šu* "flock." The following, however, will show that all the Hebrew or Amorite words had not been eliminated in the thirteen hundred years which intervened between the dates when the two tablets were written.

The word *zi-ba-ni-it* "treasures" (B, I: 33), is Amorite from the root *ṣapan* "to hide, to treasure." This root is not in current use in Akkadian.

The words *a-na pat-te* (B, I: 36) do not mean "aussitôt," nor is the reading *a-na kurmate* "for food" correct; but *pat-te* is the Hebrew word *pat* in the plural, meaning "morsels;" and the sentence reads "they prepare the child for morsels." This being a word foreign to the Akkadians, the redactor wrote the gloss which precedes, "They prepare the daughter for a meal."

The *ma* at the beginning of B, I: 43 *ma-bêl mâti* has been left wholly unaccounted for in all the translations. This is the Hebrew *waw conjunctive.*

The word *i-ri-ḫa-ma* (B. II: 50) is not Akkadian but Amorite. The word *'aruḫah* "meal, food," is found several times in the Old Testament, see Jer. 40: 5, etc.

The word *la-šu* (B, II: 56) has been construed by all the translators as the negative particle, three of whom, recognizing the difficulty, added a question mark to their conjectural translation of it; but *la-šu* is the Amorite inseparable preposition with the pronominal suffix, meaning "to him." The redactor glossed *la-šu* with the Akkadian word *it-ti-šu* which precedes.[14] In the passage which is exactly parallel (B, III: 20), it is omitted.

The word *i-ṣa-ba-ta* (B. III: 3), translated as if Akkadian from the root *ṣabâtu* "to take," makes an insurmountable difficulty; but considering that it is from the Hebrew root *'aṣab* "to grieve," see Isaiah 54: 6; I Chron. 4: 10, etc., the difficulty disappears.[14]

The word *ni-ši-tu* "desolation" (B, III:3), as referred to above in connection with *ma-ši-it-ta* of the ancient version, is Amorite.

The *me* which follows Atra-ḫasis (B, III: 29) is not an enclitic or emphatic particle attached to that name, but the Hebrew *waw consecutive*.[14] The fact that *me* is written instead of *ma* may probably be due to compensative lengthening as in Hebrew.

There are other Amorite words in the late text which are discussed in the foot notes of the transliteration and translation.

The study of the late redaction also shows that it goes back to a Hebrew or Amorite original. In no other way can the Hebrew words found in its composition be explained.

The legend had been Akkadianized before the early text was written, in 1966 B. C. In the long period which preceded it had suffered many changes when redactors had made the original Amorite text conform to the dialect in current use in Babylonia; fortunately, as we have seen, all the words peculiar to the West had not been eliminated. We see how this process went on in the writing of personal names of those coming fresh from the West in the Ḫammurabi period; for example, names like *Ishbi-Urra, Ishme-Dagan* etc., had become Akkadianized, but on the arrival from the West of others bearing those names, we find that they were written *Yashbi-Urra, Yashme-Dagan,* etc. Even the position of the verbs in the sentence had suffered changes; for while they are frequently found at the beginning, as in Hebrew, they are also found placed at the end, or indifferently in the sentence, as is the case in Akkadian.

The story of the deluge, as contained in the Gilgamesh Epic, certain scholars maintain, embraces elements of more than one tradition. They say Um-napishtim is the hero of the epic, yet it

[14] See notes beneath the word in the transliteration in the Appendix.

nevertheless also refers to Atra-ḫasis. This has prompted some scholars to identify him with Um-napishtim, while others consider that, as has already been noted, in this late story the name Atra-ḫasis is used as a synonym for "a very wise man," as is the case in several of the epics. However, it seems to the writer that the situation is entirely misunderstood. As stated above (foot note 16) Atra-ḫasis is a personal name. The passage, "the wise one, Atra-ḫasis" (B, III: 17), could hardly be translated "the wise one, the very wise;" and it doubtless shows also where the later etymologists got their idea for their play upon the name. In all the versions except the Sumerian the hero's name is Atra-ḫasis. After the flood he was given a title. Although not fully understood it is *Um*(or *Uta*)*-napishtim rûqim* (*rîgam,* also *ina rûqi*), which in the Sumerian paraphrase is written Zi-û-suddu. This title has been variously translated: "He who lengthened the days of life," "He who made life long of days," etc. Certainly this is not a personal name, which fact the Gilgamesh Story fully recognizes. When Ea (in the Gilgamesh Story E, 196) tells the gods how the hero learned that the flood would occur, he does not say, "I made Um-napishtim see a dream;" for at that time he had not been thus designated; but Ea says "I made Atra-ḫasis see a dream." That was his name; he had not yet earned the title. In short, this is no confusion of names, as some have inferred, but an exact statement. And the use of the title instead of the name in the Sumerian paraphrase is a proof that it is borrowed from the Semitic legend.

The writer has previously maintained, simply on a basis of the personal names found in the Gilgamesh Epic story, that it is largely from a Hebrew or Amorite original. Let us inquire whether a study of the language used in its composition will betray its original source.

The first Hebrew word to be noted in the Gilgamesh Epic story is *niṣirtu* "secret," (E, 9). This word, as far as known to the writer, was not in current use in Akkadian; but the Hebrew word meaning "hidden thing" from this root is known in the Old Testament (see Isaiah 48: 6, etc.).

The word for part of the boat called *la-an* (E, 60), which was the "hull" or "bottom," is Hebrew from the root *lûn* "to lodge," doubtless, because there is where the people lodged.

The word used for "the roof" of the boat, namely *ša-a-ši* (E, 60), is Amorite (see note in Appendix).

The word *qîru,* used for the outside wall of the ship (E, 66), is not Akkadian, but it is the common word for "wall" in Hebrew.

The word *sussullu* "basket" (E, 68) was not used in Akkadian but it is found in Hebrew, see Jer. 6: 9.

The root of *u-pa-az-zi-ru* (E, 70) is the common Hebrew *baṣ̣ar* "to gather, gather in, enclose."

The root of the word *e-ṣi-en-ši* "I loaded it" (E, 81) is found in all the Semitic languages except the Akkadian dialect. In Isaiah 33: 20 we have reference to "a tent that shall not be moved," i. e., "loaded."

In *pi-ḫi-i* (E, 95) is to be seen the common Hebrew word *peḫah* "governor," which was not in current use in Akkadian.

The word *ḫa-aia-al-ti* has been translated "army" (E, 131), but this is Amorite; it is not found in Akkadian.

Where one text reads *û-mu* (E, 133) the variant text reads *ta-ma-ta.* The former word has been translated "day," and the latter "sea." Certainly *ûmu* is the Hebrew *yâm* "sea," as the context and the variant clearly show.

The word *na-a-ši* (E, 142) is not Akkadian; it is from the Hebrew root *nûs* "to escape."

There are other Hebrew words discussed in the notes beneath the translations, some of which are tentatively offered, while others are reasonably certain. There are also glosses. Doubtless, further study will reveal more which were rarely, if ever, used in Akkadian. If the Um-napishtim story was originally written in Sumerian, or even in Akkadian, certainly it becomes necessary to explain how these foreign Hebrew words, even in this late version of the Assyrian period, came to be used in the Epic.

It is the writer's opinion that no other conclusion can be arrived at but that this deluge story, which probably embraces some elements indigenous to Babylonia, was mainly an Amorite legend which the Semites from Amurru brought with them from the West.

Since we know that other peoples of the early period had deluge stories, it would be precarious to say that the Sumerians and the Babylonians did not have their own, especially as this land must have suffered even more than others, and because this legend refers to Shurippak. But with this exception there is nothing in the Gilgamesh Epic story that can be said to be distinctively Babylonian. Even the word translated "reed hut" is very probably an archaic West Semitic word.[17] And on the other hand, there are, as we have seen, a number of Hebrew words used in the Epic, which were not current in Babylonia; which together with other facts show that the story is mainly Amorite. Moreover, it is not at all improbable that the reference to Dilmun in the Sumerian version, if that name is to be identified with the region of the Persian Gulf, is also a part of the local coloring the legend received after it was brought into Babylonia.

Since it has been shown that the Sumerian story, whose hero was named Zi-û-suddu, is connected with the Um-napishtim story and that it was probably written at a time when Sumerian as a spoken language had survived in a more or less corrupt style, some time between 2300 and 1300 B. C.,[18] it seems, in light of the above, until other evidence is forthcoming, the only conclusion at which we can arrive is that it must be regarded as a short paraphrase of the Amorite story, which may include some features of a Sumerian tradition. It has even taken over the Akkadian word *puḫru;* which, as we have seen, had displaced the Amorite *ḫuburu.*

The fact that Sumerian was used for official communications, for legal documents, as well as for literature in general, in certain Babylonian cities in the latter half of the third millennium B. C., makes it possible to understand why such very ancient stories, which had been brought into Babylonia from Amurru, should also be found written in Sumerian. Nearly every inscription from Nippur of this period is written in Sumerian. It was the legal and liturgical language. In some of the neighboring cities it was not so; for example, Sippara; whence probably came the ancient version of the Amorite Atra-ḫasis Epic. This city was preeminently Semitic.

[17] See note under E, 20.

[18] Poebel *Historical Texts* 66 f.

It has been claimed that the little Semitic fragment, containing thirteen partially preserved lines, now in the Museum of the University of Pennsylvania, was originally written in Sumerian, and that it was brought to Canaan at the time Abraham "left his home on the Euphrates and moved westward." But the few lines of this supposed Sumerian story are full of Hebrew words which were not in current use in Akkadian.

The word *ub-bu-ku* "overthrow" (F, 5) has not as yet been found in either language; but it is from the very common Hebrew root meaning "to overthrow," which root, excepting two substantives, was not in current use in Akkadian.

Instead of reading *lu-pu-ut-tu ḫu-ru-šu* "destruction, annihilation" (F, 5), the present writer prefers to read *lu-pu-ut-tu ḫu-ru-šu* "verily give attention to silence." The root of the latter in Hebrew means "to be silent, to be speechless." In other words, the hero is told of the proposed flood, to keep silence, and to build a ship.

The word *ga-be-e* "high" or "height" (F, 7) is found in Hebrew, Arabic, and Aramaic; but not in Akkadian.

Instead of *ba-bil* (F, 8) the reading is *ma-šum-ša* "and its name;" this contains the Amorite *waw conjunctive.*

Certainly it must be admitted that it seems strange that the Akkadian translator of this supposed Sumerian story should have used so many Hebrew words which were not in current use in Babylonia, in making the translation of these few lines into Akkadian.

The writer fully appreciates the fact that at any time cuneiform inscriptions may be found in Babylonia which will contain examples of these Hebrew words other than those already known; because of the flow of Western Semites in nearly all periods into this land; nevertheless, it will be possible to continue to maintain that they were not in current use in the Akkadian dialect.

Nearly all scholars who have published discussions of the Biblical deluge traditions in recent years have conceded that they are of Babylonian origin. This view can be said to have been very generally accepted by scholars. Some hold that these stories were brought from Babylonia to Canaan by Abraham; others say that they were transmitted to the West in the Amarna period, but the great majority of scholars hold that knowledge of them was obtained in Babylonia at the time of the exile. Two arguments are generally advanced for this position; the one is, the great age of Babylonian civilization, which involved the idea that civilization in the West had only developed a little before 2000 B. C., by Arabs from Arabia; and the other argument is based on the frequency of inundations in Babylonia, which gave rise to these so-called nature myths.

In 1909 the present writer endeavored to show that the Babylonian origin of the Biblical deluge stories was without any foundation; but that they were indigenous to the West; and that, on the other hand, the Babylonian story of the deluge, as preserved in the Gilgamesh Epic, contained West-Semitic elements; showing that no other conclusion could be arrived at, but that extensive influences had been felt from Amurru.[19] The arguments for these views were based almost entirely upon such literary evidence as the names of the gods, who are mentioned in the story, as being Amorite, as well as the name of the pilot of the ship, Buzur-Amurru.[20] In the above discussion additional proof is offered from a linguistic point of view for this thesis.

These discoveries show that there is no need to find the origin of the Biblical stories in Babylonia, because of the theory that the West in the early period did not have an indigenous literature, and did not have a civilization. The present version, and other data presented in the discussion in another chapter, forever disprove this hypothesis; and require its abandonment. Moreover, it is necessary that a general readjustment be made of views advanced by Pan-Babylonists, and Pan-Egypto-Babylonists, whose positions have been based upon the supposed Arabic origin of the Semites in Amurru; and upon the supposedly late rise and development of civilization in that land.

The discoveries made since 1909, when the present writer first contested this position, clearly show that we have reasons for believing that the civilization of the Western Semites synchronizes with the earliest that has been found in Babylonia and

[19] Clay *Amurru the Home of the Northern Semites* 71 ff.

[20] On the name Buzur-Amurru see Clay *Amurru* 82.

Egypt. More recently the writer has shown also that the theory must be abandoned that the so-called Egypto-Babylonian culture brought forth the earliest civilization in the thousand years between four thousand and three thousand B. C., while all the rest of the world continued to live in stone age barbarism or savagery;[21] for there is every reason to believe that in Amurru, with its natural agricultural districts over wide-spread areas such as those about Hit, Aleppo, Haran, etc., with its wonderfully wooded districts, as in the Lebanon region, with its mines and natural products, which in ancient times, as at present, have been so attractive for other peoples; and also in Elam, with its valleys so well adapted for agriculture, with its hills for grazing, its quarries for stone, its mines for metal, and its forests for wood; as well as in other lands in Asia, man throve before the time when through intelligence and labor, it was possible for him to control the annual floods in alluvial Babylonia, and dwell there. And further, if the Egyptian chronology of the Berlin School is correct, there is every reason to believe that in Syria there was a civilization which greatly antedated the Egyptian;[22] for, as will be seen, we now have additional discoveries that prove beyond doubt that civilization in Syria has as great an antiquity as in Babylonia. The importance of this will be readily recognized, in connection with the discovery of the Hebrew or Amorite Deluge Legend; in that it furnishes us with the background for the civilization to which it belonged; and it also makes it appear more reasonable that the Biblical legends of the deluge could be indigenous.

There is another very important fact which the old version has revealed, and that is the occurrence of *I-lu* "God," in the title of the series, as well as in the text, for the foremost deity's name. This title was originally incorrectly read *Inuma ṣallu awêlum*, and since translated many times "when a man lay down to sleep"; but *I-lu* is perfectly clear on the tablet, in the legend's context and in the colophon. *Ilu* "God" here takes the place of AN in the early Semitic and Sumerian texts, and of *Anu* of later texts. The ideogram *AN* in the early period in nearly all such connections has been generally read *Anu* or *Ana*.

[21] Breasted *Scientific Monthly* 1919, p. 577.

[22] Clay *Journal of the American Oriental Society* 41 241 ff.

It is well known that the god whose name was written with the sign *AN* "god," was the highest of the gods; who had created mankind; and who was worshipped as the supreme ruler of the universe. In the text here published, we learn that the Western Semites in this early period called the Godhead *I-lu,* or *El* "God," the same as in the Old Testament; and there can be little doubt but that in the early period, the Akkadians did the same.

It is not impossible that the Sumerians, before they came to Babylonia, called their foremost deity Ana or Anna; but there is no proof for this. To the writer it seems more probable that after they had conquered the land, and created or furnished the people with the cuneiform syllabary, they wrote *AN,* which in their language meant "heaven," as well as *dingir* "god," for the name of the most high god of the Semites, namely *Ilu.* Certainly in the early syllabaries (see below), *AN* represented *Ilu.* In time *AN* became Semitized into *Anu,* in the same way that *En-lil* "lord of the storm" became *Ellil.* It is also not improbable that the West Semitic *Anu-Ilu,* whose influence was so extensively felt in the West, even in Egypt, is the origin of the Erechian Anu.[23] Moreover, we know for a certainty that while Anu of Erech later generally replaced Ilu, this fact was fully appreciated by later generations when they used *Anu* and *Antu* with the generic sense of "god" and "goddess."

This explanation of the origin of *Anu* or *Anu(m),* also written *Annum,* and in Sumerian texts *An* and *An-nà,* and the fact that *Anu* had the meaning "god," which was pointed out many years ago, gives us reasons why the Erechian Anu "the creator," "the father of the gods," was never displaced as the head of the pantheon. And it seems that these reasons satisfactorily account for the name being written without the determinative for deity, even after the ideogram *AN* had become Babylonized into *A-num,* as is the case in the "Old Babylonian Version of the Gilgamesh Epic"; where, except *A-num,* all the gods, even the heroes, have the determinative. This can only mean that *Anu* at that time meant "god." And although the Babylonian word or name *Anu* "god" had its origin in the Amorite word or name *Ilu,* the deity

[23] See Clay *Empire of the Amorites,* 168 f.

designated by these words or names in time became quite distinct. This becomes apparent especially in periods when fresh migrations from the homeland take place.

The reading *Anu* for *AN* in the initial line of the Ḫammurabi Code is being very generally adopted; but it is a mistake.[24] When Anu of Erech is referred to in the Code, his name is written *Anum*(*-num*),[25] whereas the chief deity's name, "the father of the gods," who together with Ellil, as Ḫammurabi says, "raised the towers of Babylon," is written *Ilu*(*AN*).[26] This clear-cut distinction must be recognized. Moreover, the present text containing *ilu,* as well as the hundreds of personal names belonging to this early period compounded with *ilu,* and other facts, clearly show that the Western Semites, as well as the early Akkadians, used the word *ilu* "God" to represent their creator and supreme ruler. Naturally, this fully confirms the impression we get from the Old Testament, that the Semites, in the land called Amurru by the Babylonians, which included Aram, used the word *il*(*u*) or *el*(*u*) to designate their most high god, their *El Elyon.*[27]

Ea was not a Sumerian god, but the second in the Amorite triad, Ilu, Ea and Adad. His name was written phonetically ^{d}*E-a,* and ideographically ^{d}*En-Ki* "lord of the land," because he was Ba'al, so well known to us in the inscriptions of the West, including the Old Testament. While Ilu was supreme, Ea was the lord of the earth, of the rivers, of the springs, of the wells, and of the waters beneath the earth. It was only after the Semites had carried his worship to the southern part of the great alluvium, where a temple was erected for him at Eridu on the sea, that his cult took on the peculiar Babylonian aspect with which we are so familiar. In this alluvium, wells are dug, but springs of the

[24] Scheil originally read *ilu.* He was followed by Peiser, Winckler, Pinches, and others; but since Harper read *Anu,* not a few have followed this reading. Throughout the Code, *ilu* is used for "the god." Did the codifier in the body of the laws avoid the use of Marduk or Shamash, the god of laws, so that his code would be acceptable in places where these deities were not worshipped; or does not the use of *ilu* show rather the West Semitic origin of the Code?

[25] See 2: 46; and 44: 51.

[26] See 1: 1; 1: 31; 40: 64; 42: 45.

[27] Cf. the important contribution on the subject, Hehn *Die Biblische und die Babylonische Gotteside* 150 ff.

earth are unknown. The rivers and the rain alone bring fertility to the soil. Ea having presided over the waters of the earth naturally became in Eridu the god of the deep and of the rivers. But this is a local and a late conception of Ea, the great Amorite Ba'al. Simply because excavations have been conducted in Babylonia where the almost imperishable clay tablets have been recovered in such masses, and in Amurru little or nothing of this kind has as yet been done, where also the perishable papyrus and skin was used so extensively for writing material, is responsible for the faulty conception that exists at present not only of the god Ea, but of the entire historical situation prior to the time of Ḫammurabi.

Adad, the god of the elements, usually called the "storm god," is Hadad of Amurru, the third of the early triad. At a very early time his worship was brought into Babylonia. It is generally conceded that he is an Amorite god, and that he had been adopted as a member of the Babylonian pantheon. The ideogram ^{d}*IM* read Adad, as is well known, stands for other names of the storm-god, as Ramman, Amurru, Mar^{ki}, Mur, Sharu, etc.

At Nippur, the foremost deity was such a god as Adad. His name was written ideographically ^{d}*En-Lil,* "the lord of the storm;" which in time was used as his name, and even pronounced *Ellil.* It is possible that the Sumerians, who at an early time took possession of this city, also had a storm god; but this cannot be proved. The writer feels that ^{d}*En-Lil* was originally Adad. In the Gilgamesh Epic, he instead of Adad is the destructive god; in other words he had supplanted him after Nippur became the supreme city in the land. En-lil also displaced Ea, when he became the *bêl mâtâti,* "lord of the lands;" and thereafter he took the place of Ea as the second god in the triad; so that instead of Ilu, Ea, and Adad, the triad became Ilu(AN), Enlil, and Ea. Later, when Babylon became the centre of the hegemony, Enlil was displaced by Marduk, the god of that city, who himself became the Ba'al, or Bêl.

This forcibly recalls the fact that a large name syllabary found at Nippur, belonging to the early period, contains several groups

[23] See Chiera's important contribution on the subject, *Lists of Personal Names* 39 f.

of Semitic names compounded with those of Amorite gods. One of these groups, occurring several times, contains *AN, E-a and* ^{d}*IM*, and the other contains ^{d}*Dagan, Ishtar and Gaga;* while ^{d}*Enlil*, in whose school of scribes the tablet was written, occurs only twice among its several hundred names.[28] We have knowledge of certain syllabaries having been repeated for millenniums; and it is not impossible that this particular one was originally written prior to the time when Nippur's god became "the lord of lands"; in other words, prior to the time when the foremost triad became AN, Enlil, and Ea. Certainly we can understand why Ea, who figures in the early myths and legends in a much higher position and role than the storm-god Adad (or Enlil), originally followed the foremost deity. Yes, even in the West Semitic creation myth, Anu and Ea are the creators, while the storm-god, who is there called Marduk, fights the great Tiâmat. And we can also understand how, subsequent to the time when Nippur's Enlil became "lord of the lands," that god came to take the place of Ea next to the most high god. Moreover, it seems that conclusive proof of this position is to be found in the "Explanatory Lists of Gods." In the most ancient (II R 59), Ilu (*AN*) is followed by Ea (and his consort), and Enlil (and his consort). In the later and fuller lists, which were also written in an early period, this order is maintained, but Anu, and a consort *Antu* who was created by the force of analogy, take the place of Ilu.

In consideration of all available data, it is reasonable to conjecture that this Amorite deluge story, which preserves the names of the foremost original triad, goes back to a time as early as 4000 B. C.

II

ANCIENT FRAGMENT OF THE ETANA LEGEND

Through the discovery of dynastic lists and other historical data the great antiquity of Babylonian civilization is now fully determined. We now have lists of rulers which carry us back to the fifth millennium B. C. Instead of the earliest period known representing the beginning of civilization, there is every reason to believe that millenniums of history, not of savagery, but of civilized man, precede what we now know as the earliest; and when systematic excavations are conducted in Central Asia, in Asia Minor, and in Syria, we shall have data whereby the gap between prehistoric man of millenniums ago and man of the earliest historic period will be considerably reduced.

In the Appendix will be found the reconstructed list of ruling cities and kings. Excluding the two earliest dynasties, to the reigns of which fabulous numbers of years are given, we find ourselves at a period about 4000 B. C. (Others make the date earlier, see below.) Etana belongs to the first of the two dynasties which precede this period; which ruled in the fifth millennium B. C.

The first eight names of the earliest dynasty, namely that of Kish, are fragmentary, or are wanting. The first five that are fully preserved are Semitic; and several of these, at least, are unquestionably West Semitic. The fourth ruler, who has been heretofore regarded as mythical, is Etana; he is now restored to his place as a ruler.

It is generally understood that in certain Aryan lands gods became men. Many scholars maintain that the same has occurred with the Semites. They have said that Nimrod, the patriarchs, and many other Biblical characters were originally deities, that Etana, Lugal Marda, Tammuz, Gilgamesh and many other Babylonian rulers had also descended from the realms of mythology. Fortunately clay tablets, which are not so perishable as skins or papyrus, have recently furnished us with the material whereby some of the so-called deities are restored to their places in dynastic lists, and whereby it is possible to assert that it cannot be proved that gods ever became mortals in the Semitic world. The order must be exactly reversed. While anthropomorphic ideas are attributed to the deities, we have no instance of a Semitic god becoming a man.

This fragment of an old version of the Etana Legend was written about 2000 years earlier than the fragments found in the Library of Ashurbanipal (668-626 B. C.). It has also been previously published.[1] It contains the opening and the closing lines of a large tablet, which had three columns on the obverse and three on the reverse. It seems to the writer that the complete tablet must have contained about 275 lines. Among the fragments of the Epic written in the Assyrian period there is one which duplicates partially some lines of the present text. An outline of the legend as now known from the different fragments follows:[2]

The deity had deserted the city; and in consequence, anarchy and confusion prevailed, and productivity ceased; the sheep no longer bore young. The gods desiring to bring this state to an end designated Ishtar to go to the rescue; and Etana was installed as king. About this time an Eagle and a Serpent formed an alliance to carry on the work of destruction. Each, accompanied by a brood, went to the mountain for prey; each killed an animal; and then shared them with their broods. Although warned not to do so by one of her offspring, the Eagle pounced upon and devoured the young of the Serpent. The Serpent appealed to Shamash, the god of justice, and was advised to conceal herself in the carcass of a bull that they had slain, and when the Eagle swooped down upon it, to seize and tear her to pieces. This was done, and the Eagle was left to die in a hole in the mountain. The Eagle in turn appealed to Shamash, promising eternal obedience if rescued. Daily Etana also pleaded with Shamash to show him the "plant of

[1] Scheil *Recueil de Travaux* 23, 18 ff. A transliteration and translation on the basis of the same text was published by Jensen *KB* VI 1 100 ff, and 581 ff. See also Frank *Studien zur Babylonischen Religion* 105 ff.

[2] George Smith *Chaldean Genesis* 138 ff published the first three known fragments. E. J. Harper published seven other fragments, *BA* II 441 ff., and 503 ff. Jastrow *BA* III 379 ff, and *JAOS* 30, 101 ff, published two others. See also Jensen *KB* VI 1 100 ff. For a discussion of all the fragments, see Jastrow *JAOS* 30, 101 ff.

birth," that fertility might be restored. The god told him to seek the hole in the mountain into which the Eagle had been thrown, and there the plant would be shown him. Upon his arrival at the hole the Eagle appealed to Etana for help, promising in return to fly with him to the dwelling of the gods, probably with the idea of obtaining immortality. Etana mounted upon the back of the Eagle, and together they reached the heaven of Anu. The Eagle urged Etana to proceed to the dwelling of Ishtar, the planet Venus; but after a flight of six hours, either through exhaustion or the intervention of the goddess, a precipitous descent to the earth was made. The fragmentary character of the end of the legend leaves us in doubt whether or not it proved fatal. There can be little question but that many details of the legend are still wanting, as seems to be indicated by the art of the seal cylinders, depicting the ascent.[3]

The content of the beginning of the present text points to its being the opening part of probably the second tablet of the series which contained the legend. The closing lines refer to the resuscitation of the Eagle at the mountain hole with the assistance of Etana. Unfortunately the tablet did not contain a colophon. The fact that the last column is not completely filled out, would indicate that it was copied from a still earlier inscription. While it is not impossible that the legend was originally written in Sumerian, there is nothing in this ancient version to suggest that this was the case.

The early dynastic lists of Babylonia, given in the Appendix, show that Etana, "the shepherd," who lived in the fifth millennium B. C., was an usurper, and became the twelfth ruler of the first dynasty of Kish, who "ruled all lands."[4] In the omen text discussed below, he is called "king."

The name Etana is West Semitic, as are several of the first five rulers of the early Kish dynasty, which have been preserved. In this fragment of the early version, besides the god Anu, only the Anunnaki and the Sibitu are mentioned. In the late version many other Semitic gods are referred to, some of whom may have

[3] See Ward *The Seal Cylinders of Western Asia,* 142 ff.

[4] See Poebel *Historical Texts* p. 88.

been introduced in the later period. An interesting parallel to this is the adding of Ishtar's name as one of the gods of Eanna in the late redaction of the Gilgamesh Epic, whereas in the early version, the temple Eanna is the dwelling place of Anu alone.[5]

It is not impossible that the Etana Legend has an historical background, as in the case of the Lugal Marda, the Gilgamesh, and other epics (see below). As in the case of the so-called "Zu bird," the Eagle and the Serpent may represent two powers which were ravaging the lands, probably at a time when a famine prevailed; and upon their having difficulties between themselves, Etana aided the Eagle. His aspirations in connection with ruling all lands, whereby he would become immortal, having been urged and abetted by the Eagle, received a set-back; which allegorically is told in the story of his ascent to heaven. The power represented by the Eagle is probably to be identified with the "Zu bird" (see below), to whom the Serpent refers as a "worker of evil" in his address to the god Shamash.[6] The fact that the Serpent is told "to take the road to the mountains," and that Etana found the Eagle in a hole in the mountain, would show that the scene was not laid in Babylonia, but in a mountainous district, probably the West.

The symbol of an invader of the following dynasty, whose name was written Nin-Gish-Zidda in Sumerian, was the Serpent. The well-known goblet of Gudea with the caduceus, which in a later period was dedicated to this deified king; the bas-relief depicting this demi-god, who with heads of serpents protruding from his shoulders is leading Gudea, as well as the seal of this great patesi,[7] clearly indicate that the serpent was the emblem of Nin-Gish-Zidda. It is also not improbable that the title *ušumgal,* which can be translated "the great serpent," as well as "the great one," so frequently used in connection with titles of Tammuz, the son of Nin-Gish-Zidda, also refers to the Serpent.

The worship of the Serpent is very general in Elam, Egypt, Phoenicia, Ḫatti, Persia, India, China, and Greece. Whether in

[5] Cf. Jastrow-Clay *An Old Babylonian Version of the Gelgamesh Epic* p. 64: 58 with *KB* VI 1, 128: 37 etc.

[6] Cf. *KB* VI 1, 104: 13. This being true, the reference to Zu, the invader, being an anachronism, was added in some late redaction.

[7] See Heuzey *RA* 5, 137, and Meyer *Sumerier und Semiten in Babylonien* Taf. VII.

the early period it was so universal, or whether for the ancient period additional information will show that it was merely local, cannot be surmised. It would, therefore, seem precarious to say more than that Tammuz and his father seem to have been identified with a state the emblem of which was probably the Serpent (*ṣiru*).

In this connection we must not lose sight of the Dragon Legend (*CT* 13 33). It was after "the cities sighed" for relief when "Tâmtu the Serpent (*ṣiru*)" was the oppressor, that *ᵈSUḪ* was asked to stir up a cloud, a storm and a tempest, and by slaying the Dragon "to deliver the broad land." No one seems to hold the view that the name Tâmtu is Sumerian; and the writer feels that he has already shown there can be no question but that it is West Semitic (see *Amurru* 51ff). The Eagle probably also represented a power in the West. The transliteration and translation of the ancient fragment of the Etana Epic follow:

Ra-bu-tum ᵈAnunnaki (A-Nun-na) ša-i-mu ši-im-tim
uš-bu im-li-ku mi-li-ik ša ma-a-ta-am
ba-nu ki-ib-ra-tim ša-ki-nu ši-ki-it-tim
ṣi-ru a-na ni-ši i-lu I-gí-gu
i-zi-nam a-na ni-ši i-ši-mu
šar-ra-am la iš-ku-nu ka-lu ni-ši e-bi-a-tim
i-na lim-me-tim la ka-aṣ-ra-at ku-ub-šum me-a-nu
ù ḫa-aṭ-ṭu-um uk-ni-a-am la ṣa-ab-ra-at
la ba-nu-ú iš-ti-ni-iš pa-ra-ak-ku
si-bi-te ba-bu ud-du-lu e-lu da-ap-nim
ḫa-aṭ-ṭu-um me-a-nu-um ku-ub-šum ù ši-bi-ir-ru
ku-ud-mi-iš A-ni-im i-na ša-ma-i ša-ak-nu
ú-ul i-ba-aš-ši mi-it-lu-ku ni-ši-ša
[šar]-ru-tum i-na ša-ma-i ur-da-am
.... *i-ši-i*
ḫa-as-su iṣ-ba-ta-am si-bi-e it ...
sa-am-na-am wa-ar-ḫa-am ú-ši-te-ga šu-ut-ta-as-su
e-ru-ú ma-ḫi-ir ú-ku-ul-ta-am ki-ma ni-ši-im na-e-ri
e-mu-ga-am i-šu
e-ru-um pa-a-šu i-pu-ša-am-ma a-na E-ta-na-ma
iz-za-ga-ar-šu
ib-ri lu-ú it-ba-ra-nu a-na[-ku] ù at-ta
qi-bi-a-am-ma ša te-e-ir-ri-ša-an-ni lu-ud-di-ik-ma

E-ta-na pa-a-šu i-pu-ša-am-ma a-na e-ri-im-ma
iz-za-ga-ar-šu
i......mi-..-ti ka-ti-im-ti

The great Anunnaki who decide fate,
Sat down, took counsel concerning the land.
Builders of the quarters, the authors of nature,
The Igigi, being against the people,
Determined upon enmity for the people.
They established not a king; they shut up the people in the dwellings.
In that time(?) a headgear was not bound, a crown
And a sceptre of lapislazuli had not been possessed.
They had not built together a shrine.
The Sibitu locked the gates against the mighty.
The sceptre, crown, headgear, and staff,
As in former times, before Anu in the heavens was placed.
There is no counsel for its people.
The kingship has gone down from the heavens.
.... had ....
Took care; on the seventh ....
On the eighth month he proceeded to his hole.
The eagle having received food, like a roaring lion
Became strong.
The eagle opened his mouth, and to Etana spoke to him:
'My friend, truly we are friends, I and thou.
Command, and when thou hast cured me, I will kill.'
Etana opened his mouth, and to the eagle spoke to him:
.... covered

III

A FRAGMENT OF THE ADAPA LEGEND.

The third fragment contains a portion of the well-known Adapa Legend; but, unfortunately, it has not been possible as yet to determine in what period Adapa lived.

What is known of the legend of Adapa is based upon several fragmentary tablets which at one time belonged to the Library of Ashurbanipal (668-626 B. C.),[1] including the present text, which also had been published about twenty-five years ago,[2] and upon one that was found among the Egyptian archives of Amenophis III and IV, of the fourteenth century B. C.[3] The present text is from a fragment which contains the first part of the legend. A brief outline of the story follows, as it has been recovered up to the present.

Adapa, a semi-divine seer, who was priest of the temple of Ea, in Eridu, had been granted wisdom by his father, the god Ea, but not eternal life. One day, in exercising one of the functions of his office, namely fishing in the Persian Gulf, a sudden squall from the south upset his boat. Angered at this, he broke the wings of the south wind so that for seven days it did not blow the cooling breezes of the sea over the land. In consequence Adapa was summoned by the god Anu to appear before him in heaven. Thereupon his father Ea told him how to excite the sympathy of Gish-Zidda and Tammuz, two deified kings (see last chapter), who stood at the portals of heaven. Being cautioned by his father not to partake of the food and the drink that would be set before him, he refused; but excess of caution was responsible

[1] See K.8219, published by Strong *PSBA* 16, 274 f; and *K*.8743, published by Jensen *KB* VI 1, XVII ff.

[2] This text, and its translation were originally published by Scheil, *Recueil de Travaux* 20 (1898), 127 ff. Zimmern from a photograph, in Gunkel *Schöpfung und Chaos* 420 ff, offered several improved readings. These were utilized by Jensen *KB* VI 1, 92 ff, as well as by others. For other translations see Ungnad *ATB* I 34 ff; Barton *Archaeology and the Bible* 260 ff; and Rogers *Cuneiform Parallels* 67 ff.

[3] See Winckler and Abel *Thontafelfund von El-Amarna* No. 240; and Schroeder *VS*, 12, 194. For the transliteration and translation see Knudtzon *Die El-Amarna Tafeln* No. 356, p. 964 ff.

for his not receiving the food and water of life, whereby eternal life would have been gained.

Scholars have pointed out certain resemblances of the story to that of Adam in Genesis; and some even have contended that the Adapa Legend is the origin of the Hebrew narrative. They point to the "food of life" as corresponding to the "tree of life"; that Adapa, like Adam, had gained knowledge that was regarded as an attribute of divinity, etc. However, it was through disobedience, in order to become like God, that Adam ate of the fruit; while Adapa failed to obtain eternal life owing to his obedience to his father's counsel in not eating of it. Others have contended that Adapa and Adam are different forms of the same name; while still others hold that the name Adapa is the same as Alaparos[4] (which name they change to read Adaparos), the second of the antediluvian kings handed down by Berossus.

The present writer is inclined to believe that Adapa was what the text informs us, namely a ruler, a "sage," a "man of Eridu"; and that when excavations reveal the history of that city we shall become familiar with the history of his reign, when he will take his place with Etana, Gilgamesh, and others in the list of kings or patesis. Owing to the reference to the deified Gish-Zidda and Tammuz in the legend, although it does not necessarily follow, in view of additions made in the later redactions, the time Adapa lived may have been subsequent to the early Erech dynasty. Following is a transliteration and a translation of the fragment now in the Pierpont Morgan Library Collection.

. . . *iš-tum*
qi-bit-su ki-ma qi-bit ilu . . . . *lu-* . . . . . .
uz-na rapaštum(*-tum*) *ú-šak-lil-šu u-ṣu-rat mâti mu-lu-mu*
a-na šu-a-tu ni-me-qa iddin-šu napištam(*-tam*) *darîtam*(*-tam*) *ul iddin-su*
ina û-me-šú-ma ina ša-na-a-ti ši-na-a-ti ab-kal-lum mâr ^{al}*Eridu*
^{d}*E-a ki-ma rid-di ina a-me-lu-ti ib-ni-šú*
ab-kal-lum qi-bit-su ma-am-man ul ú-šam-sak

[4] The name Adapa is frequently written *A-da-pad.* For Alaparos = Adapa see Zimmern *KAT*^{3}, 522; King *Schweich Lectures* 1916 144; Langdon *Sumerian Epic* p. 64; Ungnad *ATB* I 39 note 1. This is a West Semitic name, and is equivalent to *Alap-Uru*, perhaps "Ox of the god Uru"; cf. *Im-me-ir-i-li* "Lamb of God," *A-ga-al-Marduk* "Calf of Marduk" *BA* VI 5, 98; see Clay *Empire of the Amorites* p. 78.

li-e-um At-ra-ḫa-si-sa ša ^{d}*A-nun-na-ki šú-ma*
ib-bu el-lam qa-ti pa-ši-šu muš-te-'-u par-ṣi
it-ti nu-ḫa-tim-me nu-ḫa-tim-mu-ta ip-pu-uš
it-ti nu-ḫa-tim-me ša ^{al}*Eridu Ki-Min.*
a-ka-la u me-e ša ^{al}*Eridu û-mi-šam-ma ip-pu-uš*
[*in*]*a ga-ti-šú el-li-ti pa-aš-šú-ra i-rak-kas*
[*in*]*a ba-lù-uš-šu pa-aš-šú-ra ul ip-paṭ-ṭar*
[^{is}] *elippa u-ma-ḫar bâ'iru-tam da-ku-tam ša* ^{al}*Eridu ip-pu-uš*
e-nu-mi-šu A-da-pa mâr ^{al}*Eridu*
[*ma-*]*ru* ^{d}*E-a ina ma-aia-li a-ina ša-da-di*
û-mi šam-ma ši-ga-ar ^{al}*Eridu iš-ša-ar*
[*ina k*]*a-a-ri el-li Kar-Sin*(*UD-SAR*) ^{is}*šaḫḫîtum ir-kab-ma*
[*ša-a-ru i*]*-zi-qan-ni-ma* ^{is}*elippi-šu iq-qi-lip-pu*
[*ina gi*]*-mu-ši-ma* ^{is}*elippi-šu ú-maḫ-ḫar*
[. . . .*ina ta*]*m-ti ra-pa-aš-ti*

. . . . . .
His word like the command of the god . . . .
Wide intelligence he perfected in him, the image of the land . . . . . .
Unto him he gave wisdom; eternal life he did not grant him.
In those days, in those years, the sage, the man of Eridu,
Ea, made him like a *riddi* among men;
A sage, whose command no one could oppose;
The mighty one, the Atra-ḫasis of the Anunaki, is he;
Blameless, clean of hands, anointer, observer of laws.
With the bakers, he does the baking;
With the bakers of Eridu, he does the baking.
The food and water of Eridu daily he provides.
With his clean hands he sets (binds) the table;
And without him, the table is not cleared (loosened).
The ship he steers; he does the fishing and hunting for Eridu.
Then Adapa, the Erechian,
The son of Ea, in retiring (?) upon the bed,
Daily the bolting of Eridu gives attention to.
In the pure rampart of Kar-Nannar, he embarked upon the sailing ship.
The wind blew, and his ship glided along.
With the oar he steered his ship.
. . . . . . upon the wide sea.

Li. 3. The text contains the sign *mu,* as Scheil originally published, and not *kul.* If *kul* is correct, it is a mistake of the scribe.

Li 17. For the restoration cf. *A-da-pa ma-ar* ^{d}*Ea. KB* VI 1, 94:11.

IV

AN EARLY CHAPTER IN THE HISTORY OF AMURRU AND BABYLONIA.

We now have considerable data for the reconstruction of a chapter in the history of Babylonia, and incidentally also that of Syria, of a very early period, namely, the second earliest known post-diluvian dynasty, which began to rule about or prior to 4000 B. C.[1] (see Dynastic List in the Appendix). There are no extant inscriptions belonging to this period that have as yet been found, but references to three of the rulers of this dynasty and their contemporaries are frequently made in later inscriptions. These furnish us with material which make it possible to rewrite a fairly complete outline of the history covering the reigns of these three important kings, Lugal Marda, Tammuz, and Gilgamesh.

The so-called "Legend of the Zu bird," found in the Library of Ashurbanipal, has been known for many years. It acquaints us with the fact that an enemy designated as "Zu the storm-bird" had robbed Enlil of Nippur of the "tablets of destiny." This, of course, can only mean his supremacy as "lord of lands." But Zu, whose name was written ^{d}Im-Dugud^{hu}, was not a bird, nor the "personification of some solar deity," but a human being, an invader, who lived in an inaccessible distant mountain.

We learn that Lugal Marda, "a shepherd," came to the rescue of the land; by some kind of strategy, succeeded in bringing back the "tablets of destiny"; and in restoring Enlil to his position. For this act he is in time credited with the title: "The Enlil of Kullab, Lugal Marda," which was adopted as the name of a star.[1a] Kullab was a part of Erech, and is doubtless where he erected his palace. It was to the "distant mountain Sâbu" that Lugal

[1] Ungnad makes the date of the beginning of the third known dynasty, that of I Ur, at 3927 B.C. (*ZDMG* 1917, 166). Meissner put it at about 3900 B.C. (*Babylonien und Assyrien* p. 23); Weidner 4148 B.C. (*MVAG* 1921 61); Legrain, 4340 B.C. (*Historical Fragments* 11).

[1a] Rawlinson, 46, 1:27.

Marda went, in pursuit of Zu. Sâbu was in the Lebanon range.[2] In other words, the enemy Zu represented an Amorite or West Semitic power, which doubtless had invaded Babylonia.[3] There can be little doubt but that the so-called "Legend of the Zu bird" was intended to commemorate the overthrow of this power by Lugal Marda. The writer has no desire to identify Zu with the power whose emblem was the eagle, but this identification is not improbable; in which case we would naturally think of the state represented by that bird in the Etana Legend (see above), and probably also in the fable concerning Gilgamesh (see below).

Years ago it was conjectured that the name Nimrod was from Nu-Marad, "man of Marad."[4] More recently another has suggested that the original form of that name was En-Marad, standing for Lugal-Marad "King of Marad."[5] It seems that he may have become En Marad "High-priest of Marad," since we know that Gilgamesh was En Kullab as well as king. We must, however, keep in mind that he was not a native of Babylonia for he was a gurum kurra "offspring of the mountains." If this "shepherd" king, who apparently was the most powerful ruler of this period, should prove to be Nimrod, his Old Testament title, "the mighty hunter," or "ensnarer," may have reference to the strategy he employed in overthrowing the so-called "Zu bird."

Lugal Marda is credited with having ruled longer than any other of his dynasty. The fragment of an historical text recently published shows that he conquered Ḫalma (Aleppo) and Tidnum in the West; and it can be assumed that he ruled the West land. This would give sufficient reason why his name should have been preserved in the traditions of the West. Nimrod is the only name of a Babylonian ruler of the early period, prior to Amraphel, that is preserved in the Old Testament. Moreover, his own habitat, or that of his ancestors, may originally have been in that land, for his wife's name, although written in Sumerian Nin-Sun, was

[2] Jensen *KB* VI 1, p. 578; Zimmern *KAT*[3] p. 574, note 3.

[3] A city Su was identified with Mari, *CT* 25, 35r 24-27. On *Su* as an element in geographical names, cf. Delitzsch *Wo lag das Paradies* p. 234 ff., and *Empire of the Amorites* p. 177.

[4] Delitzsch *Wo lag das Paradies*, p. 220.

[5] Kraeling, in Prince's article, *JAOS* 41, 201.

Semitic, namely, Rîmat-Bêlit; and her father bore the Amorite name Semak-Ur (Semachoros), a name like the Old Testament Semak-Jahu (Semachiah).[6] dNin-Sun, who became the mother of Gilgamesh (see below), bears the title *rîmtu ša supuri* in the Gilgamesh Epic.[7] This title of the queen of the great Lugal Marda has been translated by some scholars "the wild cow of the stall." Since the ideogram Sun in her Sumerian name means *rîmtu* "beloved," would not *rîmtu ša supuri* "Beloved of the fortified city," and *Rîmat-Bêlit* "Beloved of Bêlit," be somewhat more appropriate as translations for the title and name of the queen mother who dwelt in her magnificent palace, which had probably been built by her former husband, the powerful king Lugal Marda.

Tammuz followed Lugal Marda as king of Erech. It would seem that Babylonia had suffered another upheaval when Nin-Gish-Zidda, his father, had "ravaged the land"; which we learn from an omen (see below). Besides this fact the latter is known only as a deity, with his habitat at Lagash. Doubtless he had been king of that city.

Tammuz was not originally "the personification of the son of the springtime," or even "the personification of some kind of wood," as has been said, but, as the new dynastic list shows, he was a human being, and the fourth king of this early Erech dynasty.[8]

In Babylonia the legends and hymns concerning Tammuz and Ishtar are exceedingly numerous. Here they are identified especially with the city of Erech, where he ruled. From the many inscriptions relating to the cult we learn that in the fourth month, which was named Tammuz, at the time vegetation began to decay, the women mourned his death. From the cult tablets also certain facts are ascertained which enable us to know something about his family connections.

The cuneiform inscriptions inform us that the mother of Tammuz was named Zertu (which name is also written Sirdu).[9]

[6] *Empire of the Amorites* p. 84. The name is written Σευηχορος, Σακχορος, Semachoros, Sacchoros, etc.

[7] Jastrow-Clay *YOR* IV 3, 68: 236.

[8] Poebel *Historical Texts* p. 88.

[9] Cf. Zimmern *Der Babylonische Tammuz* 712.

Certainly Zertu seems to be Semitic. The name Tammuz was reproduced by two Sumerian words or ideograms, which represented the pronunciation, namely, Dumu-Zi, meaning "faithful son"; but this is no proof that Tammuz was a Sumerian. In fact the meaning of the ideograms speaks against the possibility of his being a Sumerian; "faithful son" would not be appropriate for a personal name, but rather as an epithet. His father's name, Nin-Gish-Zidda, is also in a Sumerian dress; but this very probably also represents a Semitic name. This suggestion is based on the connection of his son Tammuz with the West, and on the name of his wife Zêrtu. His having ruled at Lagash would fully account for his name being written in Sumerian. He was an invader, a fact, as already mentioned, which we learn from the omen texts.

As is well known, there are many myths and legends that have been handed down concerning Tammuz (who is also called Adonis, etc.) and Ashirta (also called Astarte, Ashtaroth, Ashtar, Ishtar, Venus, Aphrodite, etc.). The cult bearing especially upon the death and resurrection of Tammuz typified the decay of vegetation which was followed by the long dry summer, and also the revivifying of the earth in the spring. While the legends are exceedingly widespread, they are especially identified with Syria. Even in the Book of Ezekiel we learn that women sat in the temple weeping for Tammuz (8:14). Traces of the cult are handed down by the Classical writers; it is also referred to by Mandaic and Syriac writers of the post Biblical period. In Syria they cluster especially about a vale near Aphaca, at present represented by the modern 'Afqa, at the head of the wild romantic wooded gorge of the Adonis river, in the Lebanon region, midway between Byblos and Ba'albek. Here tradition says the mangled body of the hunter Tammuz was buried. Here are to be found many ruined monuments of his worship, one of which is a great temple of Astarte which Constantine destroyed. Another of the memorials that have kept the legends alive is now to be seen at Ghineh, where reliefs of Tammuz and Ashirta are carved upon the rocks. Tammuz is there portrayed with a spear awaiting the wild boar by which he was slain, while Ashirta, who mourned for him, and who, the myth tells us, descended to the underworld to deliver him from death, is seated near by in a sorrowful attitude.

The city, Ha-A, whence Tammuz came, and probably also his father, has not been located;[10] but connections of Tammuz with Syria, and especially the passage concerning him in a lamentation hymn, which reads: "at the sacred cedar, a distant place where he was born" (or "where his mother bore him"), point to the West as his birthplace.[11] Extant tradition identifies him especially with the modern Gebail, the ancient Byblos. Not a few passages, however, in the cuneiform inscriptions, show that he was especially worshipped at Ḫallab (Aleppo).[12] Certainly it would seem that his connection with Ashirta and the West would imply that he was a Semite, rather than a Sumerian. Moreover, it can be gathered from several passages that he very probably met a premature death by drowning, while associating, in the Lebanon region, with his contemporary Ashirta, who was called Ishtar in Babylonia. She seems to have been a "Queen of Sheba" or a "Cleopatra" of this early era, with her seat of government at Ḫallab.

As already mentioned, the chief seat of the cult of Ashirta, the Ashtoreth of the Old Testament, or Ishtar, in Babylonia was at Erech; but Ḫallab seems to have been her home. In one of these Babylonian lamentation hymns we have this passage: "The queen of Erech for her husband; the queen of Ḫallab for her husband (wails)." This and many other couplets referring to Ishtar or to Tammuz and Ishtar show that these two cities were intimately identified with each other. One of the earliest religious texts at present known tells us that this goddess had a shrine at Nippur and that she was from the land of Ḫallab.[13] In the Gilgamesh Epic when she proposes to Gilgamesh, king of Erech, she says: "Come, Gilgamesh, be thou my spouse. Present me with thy offspring; be thou my husband, let me be thy wife; and I will set thee in a chariot, etc. . . Into our house, under the fragrance of the cedar tree, enter. And when thou enterest our house [they shall

[10] *Empire of the Amorites* p. 83.

[11] *CT* 15, 26:5. Tradition in the West makes him the son of Cinyras of Cyprus.

[12] Scheil *RA* 8, 162, 4-5; *CT* 15, 19: 4-7; etc.

[13] Barton *Babylonian Inscriptions* I, col. 13:6. See also Poebel HGT 26: 19-20.

place thee upon] a throne; they shall kiss thy feet." Gilgamesh, in refusing her advances, asked her what she had done with her husband Tammuz, and her other husbands; whereupon she told the god Anu that Gilgamesh had upbraided her on account of her evil deeds; and she asked for vengeance.

While a temple at Adab was dedicated to Ishtar, as the brick stamp of Narâm-Sin shows, and she was worshipped in many cities in Babylonia and Assyria, Erech and Ḫallab stand out as the two cities with which she was peculiarly associated. It seems to the writer that Ḫallab is prominently mentioned in these cult tablets because that city is the home of her worship. And it is probable that it is she to whom Hammurabi refers in one of the titles he gives himself, namely, *migir têlîtum mušaklil têrîtum ša Ḫallab* "the beloved of the exalted one, who put into execution the laws of Aleppo." Since Hammurabi was an Amorite, it is not improbable that the body of his Code mainly came from that city.

Certainly, there is sufficient evidence to show that the Babylonians not only looked upon her as having been a mortal, but also upon the West as having been her habitat. Moreover, since Lugal Marda and his queen Nin-Sun, Nin-Gish-Zidda and his queen Zêrtu, Tammuz, Gilgamesh, and Ḫumbaba (see below), in other words, all the kings and queens of this period, were worshipped as deities, some of whom became very important gods, the suggestion that Ashirta, called Ishtar in Babylonia, the wife of Tammuz, had also been a mortal, seems to the writer to be perfectly reasonable. Certainly there is no available evidence to disprove this; her name does not appear in the nomenclature prior to this period. That the worship of this deified woman and her consort should have become so widespread was doubtless due not only to the nature of the cult, which has its parallels now in harvest festivals, but also to the peculiarity of it which involved disgraceful rites that appealed to the sensuality of man. Throughout Syria, including Phoenicia and Canaan, the unspeakable abominations of her licentious cult took deep root. As far as we know at present, its influence was not so general in Babylonia and Assyria, especially in the early period; the one city which seems to stand out with peculiar prominence in having temple prostitutes is

Erech. It is doubtless this fact which prompted an Assyriologist long ago to say that "Erech was essentially a Semitic city."[14] In short, in consideration of all that we know of Erech's contact with the West, where doubtless Western Semites settled at a much earlier period than in Babylonia, it is not difficult to understand how her cult migrated to the great alluvium from that region, and especially as this "Queen of Ḫallab" had become the consort of Tammuz.

Gilgamesh was connected, not with the family of Tammuz, but with that of the latter's predecessor. He was the son of Rîmat-Bêlit, the wife of Lugal Marda, and of the high priest of Kullab, a part of Erech, perhaps the Semitic quarter of that city.

There is a fable that has been handed down by Aelian that ought not to be lost sight of in this connection.[15] From it we gather that Gilgamos (Gilgamesh) was born in secret, and was thrown from the acropolis where his mother was imprisoned, and that in his fall an eagle caught him and carried him to a garden whose keeper reared him. We are led in this connection to inquire what is the significance of the legend; why is the eagle here introduced? Has it anything to do with the power represented by the eagle in the Etana legend, and perhaps also with the Zu bird in the Lugal Marda epic?

As we have seen, Tammuz and his father were identified

[14] *Gifford Lectures* 1903, p. 342.

[15] The fable of Aelian (*de Natura Animalium* 12, 21) reads as follows: It is characteristic of animals also to love human beings. For example, an eagle brought up a baby. I wish to tell the whole story, that it may bear witness to my statement. When Semachoros (Seuechoros) reigned over the Babylonians, the Chaldaeans said that the son of his daughter would take the kingdom away from the grandfather. He was alarmed at this, and if I may speak somewhat jocularly, he became an Acrisius to the girl, for he guarded her very strenuously. But, without his knowledge—for fate was stronger than the Babylonian—the girl was made a mother by a man of low degree, and bore a child. Her guards, in fear of the king, threw it from the acropolis; for it was there that the aforesaid girl was imprisoned. Well, an eagle very quickly saw the child's fall, and before it was dashed upon the earth got underneath it and received it upon his back. Taking it to a garden, he set it down very cautiously. The caretaker of the place, seeing the pretty child, was fond of it and reared it; it was called Gilgamos, and reigned over the Babylonians. If anybody thinks this a fable, I admit that on testing it I thought lightly of its validity myself. But I am told that Achaemenes, the Persian, from whom the Persian nobility descends, was an eagle's nursling. (Translated from the Greek by Prof. A. M. Harmon.)

with the emblem of the serpent. Are we to understand that perhaps Gilgamesh, the son of the former queen, Rîmat-Bêlit, when born, perhaps during the reign of Tammuz, was secretly carried away and reared in the land which the eagle represents? When Rîmat-Bêlit said to her son concerning Engidu, "Some one, O Gilgamesh, who like thee in the field was born, and the mountain has reared, thou wilt see",[16]—does this imply such an order of events? What was the affinity that was responsible for Gilgamesh and Engidu being drawn together? We read in the Ninevite version these words: "Ere thou camest down from the mountain, Gilgamesh beheld thee in a dream." When the expedition to the West was being planned, Engidu said: "Know, my friend, when I moved about with the cattle in the mountains, I penetrated to the distance of a double measure into the heart of the cedar forest where Ḫumbaba lived." He knew "the paths through the cedar forest"; and it seems reasonable to ask whether the nation, whence he came, is not to be identified with the power whose emblem was the eagle.

We are led to believe from the Epic of Gilgamesh that in the early part of his career, Erech was subservient to another throne, and we inquire whether it can be ascertained what power had humiliated Babylonia at this time.

The character Ḫumbaba in the Epic has not been regarded as historical. He has been looked upon as a mythical personage who played a part in a nature myth which had been woven into the exploits of Gilgamesh. Engidu is another mythical character who has been regarded as "a type of primaeval man." The stronghold of Ḫumbaba, with whom Gilgamesh fought, as related in the epic, has in the past generally been located in Elam; and it has also been generally held that his name is Elamitic. These conclusions have not rested upon the fact that cedar forests were known to have existed in Elam; for all the numerous references to cedars in the inscriptions have been understood to refer to the Lebanon and Amanus ranges.

The conclusions that Ḫumbaba was Elamitic, and that the scenes took place in Elam rested solely upon the slight resemblance of

[16] See Jastrow-Clay *YOR* IV 3, 62: 17.

the name Ḫumbaba to that of the well known Elamite god Ḫumba, whose name was variously written Ḫumman, Ḫumba, Ḫumban, Umman, Umba, etc. The identification of Ḫumbaba with this deity was also one of the reasons why emphasis was placed upon the Gilgamesh Epic being based upon a foundation of myth, being in part astral, and in part a nature myth. A comparison of the name was made with Kombabos of the Legend of Lucian, concerning the building of the temple at Hierapolis; but the name continued to be identified with the Elamite god.[17] Others realized that the description of the cedars seemed to suggest the districts in the West; nevertheless the forests were considered to be in Elam.[18] In the light of what follows, however, this must be abandoned.

In the omen literature there is a word which has been read *ḫu-pi-pi*. It occurs several times, and has been generally regarded to be the name of an animal; it has even been translated "hyena."[19] The same word occurs as a personal name in the temple administrative archives of the early period. This word, strange to say, has also been regarded as an Elamitic loan-word, but on the basis of the reduplication of the final consonant.[20]

A few years ago an Amorite Name-Syllabary was published which had been excavated by Haynes at Nippur, and which contained the personal name *Ḫu-pi-pi*.[21] More recently there was discovered in the Yale tablet of the old Babylonian version of the Gilgamesh Epic, that the familiar name Humbaba, or Hubaba, is written exactly the same, namely *Ḫu-PI-PI*. Since the sign *PI* has also the value *wa*, and *wa* and *ba* in this period interchange, the correct reading of the word in the omen texts, and of the personal name, was not *Ḫu-pi-pi*, but it was *Ḫu-wa-wa;* and this reproduced the pronunciation of *Ḫu-ba-ba*.

It followed from this discovery that the name was the same as that of Hobab, the father-in-law of Moses (Num. 10:29); and

[17] Ungnad-Gressmann *Das Gilgamesch-Epos* p. 77.
[18] Ungnad-Gressmann *ibidem* p. 111.
[19] Holma *Namen der Körperteile* p. 151, note 2.
[20] Weidner *OLZ* 17, p. 502.
[21] Chiera *Lists of Personal Names* p. 122.

since it unquestionably was Amorite or West Semitic, there could be little doubt but that it was the same as Kombabos of Lucian.[22] Furthermore, it naturally followed that the reference to the conflict between Gilgamesh of Erech and Ḫubaba or Ḫumbaba of the West was an allusion to an important historical event of the early period.[23] Additional light is now thrown upon the situation from a passage in an omen text in the Pierpont Morgan Collection (see below), which fully substantiates the inferences which the writer made.

It is a well established idea that the definite historical allusions to which omens refer, were originally supplied by actual events that followed the appearance of the prognosticating signs which the priests had observed. Following are a few of the omens referring to historical events:

"If the foetus is male and female (a monstrosity), it is the omen of Bau-ellit, who ruled the land; the king's country will be seized."[24] It is now definitely known that this woman, Bau-ellit, overthrew the rule of Akshak, and established the fourth dynasty of Kish.

No less than eleven historical omens are known which bear upon Sargon's reign. In one of them the expression "he possessed no foe nor rival," meaning that he had subdued the neighboring lands, is fully borne out by many discoveries.

There are two well known omens relating to Narâm-Sin, one referring to his overthrow of Apirak, and the other to his conquest of Magan. The former is summarized in the eighteenth line in the Morgan text, which reads: "If the *tirani* is like a woolen rope, it is the omen of Narâm-Sin, who overthrew Apirak in arms." This is fully confirmed by the chronicles of Babylonian kings.[25]

Another omen referring to the founder of a dynasty reads: "If a sheep gives birth to an ox, etc., it is the omen of Ishbi-Urra, who did not have a rival."[26] We now have historical data to show

[22] It is not improbable that Lucian's tradition contains a reflection of the ancient Ḫumbaba, who may have built or rebuilt the temple.

[23] *Empire of the Amorites* p. 88.

[24] *CT* 28, 6: 1 f.

[25] King *Chronicles* I, 32 ff.

[26] *CT* 27, 22: 21.

that this Amorite, from the city of Mari, overthrew the third dynasty of Ur, and became the founder of the Nîsin dynasty.[27] These examples suffice to show that omens of this character unquestionably refer to historical events, and notably to great conquerors who overthrew dynasties, as well as to subjugating enemies.

The two omens referring to Ḫuwawa have been known for some time; one reads: "If a woman give birth to the face of Ḫuwawa; the king and his sons will leave the city."[28] The other is: "If a sheep bear a lion, and it has the face of Ḫuwawa, the prince will not have a rival; he will destroy the land of the enemy."[29] In an omen text of the Pierpont Morgan Collection (BRM IV, 13), the following is found in line 65: "If the *tirani* is like the face of *ᵈḪum-Ḫum,* a usurper of the land will rule the world." A fragment in the British Museum duplicates the first part of six consecutive lines of this text (i. e., 63 to 68), the third of which reads: "If the *tirani* is like the face of *Ḫum-ba-ba,*" etc.,[30] showing that the ideogram *ᵈḪum-Ḫum* is to be read *Ḫumbaba* or *Ḫuwawa.* These omens can only be interpreted as meaning that Ḫumbaba was a usurper, who like Bau-ellit, Sargon, and Ishbi-Urra, overthrew a dynasty, conquered the lands, and was without a rival. The third interprets the other two; together they clearly indicate that Ḫumbaba or Ḫuwawa had been a mighty conqueror, and that he had doubtless subjugated Babylonia.

What the characteristic feature was which enabled the priests to associate the omen-sign with Ḫuwawa is not clear. Jastrow has shown that Ḫuwawa in omens is contrasted with *tigru* "dwarf."[31] The character of Ḫuwawa or Ḫumbaba is described in the Gilgamesh Epic as *dapini* "terrible one," "whose roar is a deluge, whose mouth is fire, whose breath is death." The elders in their effort to dissuade Gilgamesh from attempting to overthrow him, asked: who has ever penetrated to his dwelling place

[27] *Empire of the Amorites* p. 107.
[28] *CT* 27, 3: 17; 4: 9; and 6: 4.
[29] *CT* 27, 21: 8. See also *CT* 28, 14: 12. Cf. also *Ḫu-um-ba-bi-tu CT* 27, 4: 8.
[30] Boissier *Divination* p. 91.
[31] *Religion Babyloniens* II, 913 f.

or capital in the heart of the cedar forest? Who has ever opposed his weapon? In short, the references to the despot seem to convey the idea that he was a powerful personage.

Gilgamesh figures also in the divination texts; among which the following has been found: "If a woman give birth, and the (child) has the head of a snake; (it is) the omen of Nin-Gish-Zidda who ravaged the land; (and it is) the omen of Gilgamesh who ruled the land, and who became 'the king of hosts' in the land."[32] It is clear from the Gilgamesh Epic that Gilgamesh in the early part of his reign was subservient to another, and that he was able to overthrow the enemy.

We learn therefore from the omen texts that one named Ḫumbaba, who had usurped the throne of the West, had conquered the land; and we learn from the Gilgamesh Epic that about this time a personage named Engidu, which Sumerian name was very probably originally Semitic, Ea-ṭâbu or Ba'al-ṭôb, appeared on the scene and became the ally of Gilgamesh. Possibly we may later ascertain that the power which Ḫumbaba represented was designated by the eagle. At present, however, this can only be regarded as conjectural. Moreover, the epic bearing the name of Gilgamesh was originally written to commemorate the overthrow of Ḫumbaba, which when accomplished doubtless enabled Gilgamesh to become the 'king of hosts.'

The fact that Ḫumbaba, who bears an Amorite name, is a historical personage, that he lived in a cedar district of the West, and that he humiliated Babylonia at the time of Gilgamesh, about 4000 B. C., prove conclusively the writer's contentions concerning the antiquity of the Amorite civilization.

Among the historical documents found at Nippur, there has come to light more than one effort on the part of ancient scribes, who lived prior to the time of Abraham, to give a history of the world, beginning with a creation story, the building of cities, a deluge story, and dynastic lists extending to the time the tablets were written. Unfortunately nearly all tablets of this period have come down to us in a fragmentary condition. They, however, forcibly remind us of the efforts of the Biblical writer; and give us the know-

[32] *CT* 27, 1: 8-9.

ledge that the Babylonians also had outline histories of man from the beginning. Moreover, the knowledge that the Babylonians had several creation myths, and more than one version of the deluge, parallels what the literary analysis of the Pentateuch had long ago determined, namely that in the Old Testament there are two creation stories and two of the flood, as well as other duplicate traditions, such as are found in Babylonian libraries. And further, the discovery that the Atra-ḫasis Epic is of Amorite origin gives us another West Semitic or Hebrew tradition of the deluge.

There would seem to be little doubt that the names of the patriarchs, which are given in the Old Testament, belong to the Hebrew or the Aramaean branch of the Semitic race; and that other lists of contemporaneous rulers among the Semites were also in existence. The antediluvian list of kings handed down by Berossus is one of these. All kinds of efforts have been made to show that the Hebrew list is taken from this one; but they have utterly failed. They have in common only one thing, that is the tenth antediluvian in each list is a hero of the flood, in one case Noah, and in the other Atra-ḫasis. If it should be found that the Amorites of Mesopotamia used clay for their writing material in the early period, it is highly probable that in time similar lists will be found. Certainly the discoveries made in Babylonia would indicate that lists of rulers and similar traditions existed in the library of every great temple.

The second important result of these discoveries is the realization of the fact that underlying the Old Testament outline of history, as well as these chronicles of the Babylonians, there is real history. The claim that the Biblical patriarchs and the early kings of Babylonia are the creation of a fiction writer, or belong to mythology, has no support from the discoveries made in the past decade. In every instance in which archaeology has thrown light upon the subject, we find that we have historical characters to deal with. There may be only a few names given, and they may be made to represent a period which actually covered many millenniums of history, nevertheless, there are reasons for believing that the names represent actual persons who lived. Man may be depicted as riding to heaven on the back of an eagle, turning into a pillar of salt, fighting with an angel, or living in a whale's belly for three days, but nevertheless we have reasons to believe that their names represent historical characters. Again and again have we had the experience of transferring names from what has been regarded as the realm of mythology, or what has been regarded as the creation of an ancient fiction writer, to the pages of history. The discoveries of the past decades have played such an important role in this connection that it is now possible to assert that it is impossible for those scholars who relegate to the region of myth certain Biblical or Babylonian characters to substantiate their position. In short, as already stated, it cannot be shown from the literature of the ancients that in the Semitic world a single god ever became a mortal. We find a process analogous to what took place in Greece and elsewhere; epics and traditions were directly based upon historical personages; moreover, many deities have already turned out to be deified persons, especially kings.

Prior to 1909, when the present writer first contested this general position, it had been demonstrated that the Ḫammurabi dynasty was Amorite, with the understanding, however, that Amorites were Arabs. Those who held the view that the periodic Arab migrations accounted for the peoples in Syria, Mesopotamia, and Babylonia, maintained that an early wave furnished Babylonia with Semites late in the fourth millennium B. C., that a second wave between 2400 and 2100 B. C. furnished Syria and Mesopotamia with Amorites; that between 1500 and 1300 a third wave furnished Palestine and adjacent lands with Aramaeans and Hebrews; and that in the seventh century of the Christian era, Western Asia and Europe received Arabs, namely Mohammedans. Another who accepted and promulgated the theory completed the thousand year "spilling over" process by inserting another wave from the fifth century B. C., when Nabataeans moved upon Petra; in short, these periodical outbursts or "sporadic waves of hungry tribesmen," occurring about every thousand years when Arabia became so full that this spitting out process was necessary, furnished Syria, Mesopotamia, and Babylonia with its inhabitants.

In *Amurru the Home of the Northern Semites* (1909), and more recently in *The Empire of the Amorites* (1919), the writer contested this theory, as accepted by many adherents, largely on the basis of a study of the nomenclature found in the Babylonian inscriptions. Hundreds of data were offered in proof of the new position, some of which were facts, others were based upon different interpretations, or upon what seemed to be implied, and, as would be expected, upon suggestions which had no direct bearing upon the thesis, but which seemed to throw light upon the historical background of these peoples. While admitting that Arabs have in all periods filtered into these lands, the writer contends that this wave theory is baseless; and he has presented many discoveries to show that the civilization of Syria and Mesopotamia, that is, the land of the Amorites, synchronized with the earliest known in Babylonia and Egypt. Some additional discoveries were presented in an article on the Antiquity of Babylonian Civilization published in 1921, which are augmented in the present treatise. In short, while an abundance of material has been discovered during the past decade which permits of the gradual reconstruction of the history of Amurru, and which tends to confirm the writer's position, he knows of nothing that has come to light which supports the contested theories.

In conclusion, the writer's position is summarized in the following two points, both of which imply the negation of prevailing theories.

First, while Arabs have always filtered into adjacent lands there is no basis for the theory that within the period covered by the written history of man, the inhabitants of Syria, Mesopotamia, and Babylonia were dependent upon Arabia for their Semites and their culture; on the contrary, the Semites in Syria and Mesopotamia had an indigenous existence and civilization which synchronizes with the earliest known in Babylonia and Egypt.

Second, that the position of the Pan-Babylonists, namely that Israel's culture and religion was of Babylonian origin, is without foundation, for the culture is indigenous, excepting the interchange of cultural elements which ordinarily takes place between neighboring peoples; on the contrary, the Semites of Babylonia came into the great alluvium pre-eminently from Syria and Mesopotamia, as is echoed in the tradition "and it came to pass as they journeyed eastward that they found a plain in the land of Shinar;" and they brought with them their religion and culture which, under the influence of the Sumerians, resulted in what we call Akkadian or Semitic-Babylonian. These two points summarize the writer's position.

APPENDIX.

A. AN EARLY VERSION OF THE ATRA-ḪASIS EPIC.[1]

Transliteration.	Translation.
	Column I.
[*li*]-*'*(?)-*bi-il* [*ri*]-*ig*-[*ma-ši-i*]*n bal-ṭi-a*(?)	I will bring(?) their clamor(?).......
ma-tum ir-ta-bi-iš ni-[*šu im*]-*ti-da*	The land had become great; the people had multiplied.
[*m*]*a-tum ki-ma li-i i-ša-ab-bu*	The land like a bull had become satiated.
[*i-na*] *ḫu-bu-ri-ši-na i-lu it-ta-aḫ-da-ar*	[In] their assemblage God was absent.
[......] *iš-te-me ri-gi-im-ši-in*	...... heard their clamor.
[*iz*]-*za-kar a-na el*(?)-*li ra-bu-tim*	He said to the great gods(?),
iq-ta-ab-ta ri-gi-im a-wi-lu-ti	Those observing the clamor of men,

[1] Scheil *Recueil de Travaux* 20 55ff; Jensen *Keilinschriftliche Bibliothek* VI 1 288 ff; Dhorme *Choix de Textes Religieux Assyro-Babyloniens* 120ff; Ungnad *Altorientalische Texte und Bilder* I 57f; and Rogers *Cuneiform Parallels* 104ff.

A, 4. The word *ḫu-bu-ri-ši-na*, which occurs several times in the redaction, was left untrans- lated by all except Dhorme, who rendered it "totalité." The root of this word in Hebrew and Aramaic means "to join, to associate;" cf. חֶבֶר "company, association;" חָבֵר "asso- ciate, companion." The corresponding word in Babylonian was *puḫru*, which the redactor employed in his paraphrases.

A, 4. The only root in Hebrew or Aramaic to which *it-ta-aḫ-da-ar* could belong is עדר "to be absent, lacking." I am indebted to Professor Torrey for this identification. It is probable that a redactor did not understand the word, for he changed the thought in his para- phrase, and used a word similar in appearance, *eli rigmešina ittadir* "concerning their clamor he was troubled."

A, 5. *dEn-lil* is probably to be restored (see note under B, III:4). It is to be regretted that one of the three passages (see also B, III:37) does not preserve the name intact.

A, 6. The words *el*(?)-*li ra-bu-tim* are replaced in the late redaction by *ana ilâni mârê-šu* "to the gods, his children" (see B, III:5).

A, 7. *Iq-ta-ab-ta*, written [*iq*]-*tab-ta-ma* in the redaction (B, III:6), seems to be from the root עקב "to trace, investigate, search out." It is found in all the Semitic languages except Akkadian. In Hebrew it especially means "to follow at the heel." Cf. the form *i-ṣa-ba-ta* (B, III:3), which was used in the redactor's paraphrase.

i-na ḫu-bu-ri-ši-na iz-za-kar ma-ši-it-ta	In their assemblage he spoke of desolations.
[lip-par]-sa a-na ni-ši te-i-na	Let the fig tree for the people be [cut off].
[i-na-ša-da]-ti-ši-na li-'-zu ša-am-mu	[In] their [fields], let the plant become a weed(?)
...... *šu ᵈAdad li-ša-aq-ṭi-il*	...... the sheep let Adad destroy.
ḫi-bi-iš -*a [li]-il-li-ka*	Injured. [The fountains of the deep] let not flow.
[ia iš-ša-a me-li na]-aq-bi	[That the flood rise not at the so]urce.
[li]-il-li-ik ša-ru	Let the wind blow.
[na]-ag-bi-ra li-e-ir-ri	Let it drive mightily.

A, 8. The root of *ma-ši-it-ta* is the Hebrew שׁוא "to devastate, to be desolate," a root which is parallel in meaning to שׁאה; cf. מַשֻּׁאוֹת Psalm 74.3, and also the noun שְׁאֵת, as well as שְׁאִיָּה "desolation," Is.24:12. Compare *ni-ši-tu* in the redactor's paraphrase (B, III:3), which is somewhat similar in meaning. In V R 31:30 *maš-ši-ti* is parallel to *ni-ši-tum*. These have been construed as meaning "to forget" from the Akkadian *mašû*, see Delitzsch *HWB* 486a. However, it must be said that there is a possibility of *mašittu* being identified with *mašâdu* "to press, oppress, strike."

A, 9. This is the Amorite word תְּאֵנָה meaning "fig tree;" in the redaction the Akkadian *tîtu* is used (see also Chap. I).

A, 10. The root of *li-'-zu* is not known to the writer. In B, III:43 the same expression is found where *li-me-ṣu* is used; see also *e-me-ṣu* B, III:53. It would appear that the root is not *amâṣu* "to be little, wanting," but *maṣû* or *waṣû*. The context suggests that perhaps the verb was a denominative, meaning something like "to become weeds, thorns;" cf. *ṣeru palku lûlid idranu* (B, III:4) "let the wide field bear weeds(?);" which the gloss probably indicates was not understood by the scribe of the late text (see below). The writer tentatively restores *[i-na ša-da]-ti-ši-na* (שָׂדֶה), instead of *karšišina* as in the redaction, because he feels the redactor in writing the paraphrase did not understand the passage.

A, 11. Scheil originally regarded the root of *li-ša-aq-ṭi-il* as meaning "to kill;" this is Hebrew. The form *lišaqṭil* should be noted. As already stated, similar forms are found in the text, like *lišaznin*, etc.

A, 12. The words which appeared in the line before the text was injured were perhaps the Hebrew מַעְיְנֹת תהום, written *e-na-at ta-ma-ti* "fountains of the deep." Since the parallel passage B, III:45 has *li-is-sa-kir*, probably this word stood also in the original text instead of *[li]-il-li-ka*, which would give us a line parallel to Gen. 8:2, where the same verb is used.

A, 13. This passage is restored with the help of the late text, B, III:45 and 55.

A, 15. *[na]-ag-bi-ra* seems also to be Amorite from the root גבר; cf. גִּבּוֹר "mighty."

A, 15. The root of *li-e-ir-ri* is to be found in the Hebrew ירה "to throw, hurl." It has been suggested by Professor Torrey that this may be the root of *ur-ru-u ša šâri*, see Delitzsch *HWB* p. 130b.

[*ur*]-*bi-e-tum li-im-ta-an-ni-ma*	Let the clouds be held back, that
[*zu-un-nu i-na šamê*] (-*e*) *ia it-tu-uk*	[Rain from the heav]ens pour not fort
[*li-šu*]-*ur eqlu iš-bi-ki-šu*	Let the field withhold its fertility.
[*li-ni-'*] *ir-ta ša* ^{d}*Nisaba*	[Let a change come over] the bosom Nisaba.

Column II.

li-.	Let . . . .
li-ba-aš.	Let . . . .
li--ša-aq-ṭi-il . . . . *ga-az*	Let him destroy . . . .
i-na še-ri-im ib-ba-ra li-ša-az-[*ni-in*]	On the morrow let him cause it to rai mightily
li-iš-ta-ar-ri-iq i-na mu-ši. . . .	Let him give in the night . . . .
li-ša-az-ni-in na-aš-[*ba*	Let him cause it to rain a tempest. . . . .
eqla ki-ma ša-ar-ra-qi li-ba-a li.	Let it come upon the field like a thie Let . . . . . .
ša ^{d}*Adad i-na a-li ib-nu-u bi*	Which Adad had created in the city . . .
iq-bu ma-iz-zu-u na-gi	They cried out and became furious . . .
ri-ig-ma u-še-lu	They sent up a clamor . . . .
ú-ul ip-la-ḫu.	They feared not . . . .

Column VII.

i	. . . .
^{d}*En-ki*	Ea . . . .
^{d}*En-ki bi-a-šu* [*i-pu-ša-ma*]	Ea his mouth [opened and]
iz-za-kar a-na i	Spake to . . . .
a-na mi-nim tu-ta-am-ma-	Why hast thou commanded . . . .
ú-ub-ba-al ga-ti a-na n[*i-ši*	I will stretch out my hand to th pe[ople] . . . .
a-bu-bu ša ta-ga-ab-bu	The flood, which thou hast ordered . . . .

A, 16. The root of *li-im-ta-an-ni-ma* is evidently the familiar Hebrew מנע "to withhol hold back;" used of rain, Amos 4:7; of showers, Jer. 3:3; etc. I owe this identification t Professor Torrey.

A, 17. This and the following two lines are restored from the late redaction; see B, III:4 47, 56 and 57.

A, 18. The meaning "Ertrag, produce," etc., have been offered for *išbiku* (see Jensen *K.* VI 1 278 note 8). In Hebrew, the root besides the general meaning "to pour out" mean also "to shed blood," "to pour out one's soul, one's personality."

A, 70. The word *ib-ba-ra* apparently is Amorite; cf. the Hebrew אַבִּיר "mighty."

A, 75. It seems as if *ma* is *waw consecutive.*

ma-an-nu šu-ú a-na-ku	Who is he? I ....
a-na-ku-ma ú-ul-la-da	I truly will bear ....
ši-bi-ir-šu i-ma-aš-ši-id	His work he shall suppress ....
li-ib-te-ru šu-ú	Let be restrained; ....
ilu-šu ul-la-ad ù iltu	His god will bear; and his goddess(?) ....
li-il-li-ku i-na [^{iṣ}*elippi*	Let them go into the [ship]
ta-ar-ku-ul-li pi-ir	The ship-mast ......
li-il-li-ku	Let them go ......
li-ir-	......
mu	......

COLUMN VIII.

.... *na ù*	....
.... *ga-me-ir*	....
.... *ra* .... *a-na ni-ši i-pu-uš*	...... for the people he made
^{m}*At-ra-am-ḫa-si-is bi-a-šu i-pu-ša- m*[*a*]	Atram-ḫasis opened his mouth, and
iz-za-kar a-na be-li-šu	Spoke to his lord.
37	37 (lines)
duppu II $^{kam-ma}$ *i-nu-ma i-lu a-wi-lum*	The second tablet (of the series) "When God, man."
šu-nigin-bi 439	Its total is 439 (lines)
qât Azag-^{d} *Aya dup-sar ṣiḫru*	By the hand of Azag-^{d}Aya, the junior scribe.
^{arḫu}*Šabatu ûmu 28*^{kam}	Month Shebet, day 28th
mu Am-mi-za-du-ga lugal-e	of the year when Ammi-zaduga, the king,
bad Am-mi-za-du-ga^{ki}	built the city Dûr-Ammi-zaduga
ka ^{id}*Buranuna*^{ki}*-ra-ta*	at the mouth
in-ga-an-dim-ma-a	of the Euphrates (11th year).

B. A LATE REDACTION OF THE ATRA-ḪASIS EPIC.[2]

TRANSLITERATION.	TRANSLATION.

COLUMN I.

[*II*] *ša*[*ttu*] [*i-na ka-ša-di-šu*]	[When] the second year [arrives]......
[*III*] *šattu* [*i-na ka-ša-di*]	[When] the third year [arrives]......

A, 398. The root of *tarkullu* רגל or רכל was not in current use in Akkadian.

[2] The text is published in *CT* 15, 49; it was translated by Zimmern *ZA* 14 277ff; Jensen *KB* VI 1 274ff; Dhorme *Choix* 128ff; Ungnad *ATB* I 61ff; and Rogers *Cuneiform Parallels* 104ff.

ni-šú i-na .... ši-na it-tak-ru	The people in their ... become changed.
IV šattu i-na ka-[ša-di]-šú ma-za-zi-šú-nu ik-ru-ni	When the fourth year arrives, their position was miserable.
rap-ša-tu .... ši-na is-si-qa	The wide ... their ... became oppressed.
qa-da-qad .... [it-tal]-la-ka ni-šú i-na su-qi	The people [wan]der in the streets with the head [bowed].
V šattu i-na ka-ša-[di] e-rib ummi mârtu i-da-gal	When the fifth year arrives, the daughter looks for the entering of the mother.
ummu a-na mârti ul i-pa-te bâbi-[ša]	The mother opens not [her] door to the daughter.
zi-ba-ni-it ummi mârtu i-[na-ṭal]	The daughter [looks] upon the treasures of the mother.
zi-ba-ni-it mârti i-na-ṭal [ummu]	[The mother] looks upon the treasures of the daughter.
VI šattu i-na ka-ša-di il-tak-nu ana nap-t[a-ni mârta]	When the sixth year arrives, they prepare the [daughter] for a meal.
a-na pat-te bu-na il-tak-nu : im-la-ni ma-	For morsels they prepare the child ... were full(?)....
bîtu il-ta-nu šanû(-ú) i-[ri-ḫa-ma]	One house [devours] another.

B, I:28. Dhorme reads *ma-ḫa*(or *za*)*-ṣi-šu-nu,* and translates "leurs villes(?)," and i followed by Rogers; Jensen and Ungnad leave untranslated.

B, I:30. The first part of the line is read *qa-ṭ(d)a is(ṣ,z)-?* by Jensen; *qa-da-iṣu* by Dhorme, and *qa-da-niš by Rogers.* It is not improbable that the third sign is *qad,* in which case the first word would be *qa-da-qad* = Hebrew קָדְקֹד "crown of the head."

B, I:33. It seems to the writer that the root of the word *zi-ba-ni-it* "scales" is the צפן "to hide, treasure up," which was not in current use in Akkadian. "Treasured things, stores" would make better sense than "scales", as usually translated, in the above passage. Th word *ṣapanišu* occurs in the Amarna Letters. Knudtzon translates *u i-za-ḫar i-na ṣa-pa-ni-š* "und wiederkehrt bei seinem Verschwinden" (147:10). This, the writer suggests, shoul be translated "who is mindful of his treasure."

B, I:36. The words *a-na pat-te* have been translated by Dhorme "aussitôt," by Ungnad "zur Zehrung(?)," perhaps reading *kurmate*(*-te*), who is followed by Rogers reading *a-na pat-t* "for food(?)." The word seems to be the Hebrew פַּת "morsel." Not being current i Babylonia and Assyria the redactor wrote the gloss which precedes: "they prepare th daughter for a meal."

B, I:37. The word *i-ri-ḫa-ma* restored from II:50, is Amorite, although the only occurrenc of the root in the O. T. is in אֲרֻחָה "meal, food" (Gesenius *Heb. Dic.* 17 p. 65). The roo *arâḫu* occurs in IV R 49, 29b, and is explained as meaning *akâlu* "to eat," cf. Delitzsch *HW* p. 132.

ki-i še-dim-me-te pa-nu-ši-na [*kat-mu*]	Like ghosts their faces [they cover].
ni-šu i-na šu-par-ki-e [*napišti bal-ṭa-at*]	The people [live] in violence.
šipra il-qu-[*u*]	They took a messenger ....
e-tar-bu-ma	They entered, and ......
te-ir-ti	An oracle ....
ma-bêl mâti... 44...*ta-ia-a-*[*ru*].... 45.... *ma*.... 46.... *ma*	And the lord of the land .... the return ......

Column II.

ši ...... 28 *iṣ-ṣur*	.... bird........
e-liš [^{d}*Adad zu-un-na-šu u-ša-qir*]	Above [Adad made scarce his rain].
is-sa-kir šap-[*liš ul iš-ša-a me-lu i-na na-aq-bi*]	Be[low] (the fountain of the deep) was stopped, [that the flood rose not at the source].
iš-šur eqlu [*iš-pi-ki-e-šu*]	The field diminished [its fertility].
[*i-ni-' irtu ša*] ^{d}*Nisaba* [*: mušâti*^{meš} *ip-ṣu-u ugarê*^{meš}]	[A change came over the bosom of] Nisaba. [By night the fields became white].
[*ṣêru pal-ku-u u*]*-li-id id-*[*ra-nu*]	[The wide plain] bore weeds(?).
[*šam-mu ul u-ṣa*]*-a šú-*[*u ul i'-ru*]	[The plant came not] forth; the sheep [did not become pregnant].
[*iš-ša-kin-ma a-na nišê*^{meš} *a-sa-ku*]	[Calamity was put upon the people].
[*rêmu ku-ṣur-ma ul u-še-šir šir-ra*]	[The womb was closed, and the child came not forth].
....	[..............]

B, I:38. Jensen reads *ki-i simti: simāti* "gemäss dem, was gehörig ist," Dhorme *ki-i simāti* "au lieu .... ? d'ornaments." Ungnad and Rogers leave untranslated. For *šedimmu* and *idimmu* "ghost" see Muss-Arnolt *Dic.* 1016a.

B, I:39. Jensen reads *šu-ut(-)k(q)e-e-zi bal-ṭa-at* without translating. Dhorme reads *šu-par-ki-e napišti bal-ṭa-at* "Les gens vivaient d'une vie éteinte." Ungnad did not translate, and Rogers followed *Dhorme,* translating "the people lived with bated breath." The root *parâku* "to display violence" is used in Akkadian.

B, I:43. This *ma* is left wholly unaccounted for in the translations. The writer proposes that it is the *waw conjunctive.*

B, II:33. Different meanings have been offered for the word *idranu,* as "ashes, alkali, saltpeter, salt, weeds, thorns." For the latter see Hinke *A New Boundary Stone of Nebuchadnezzar* p. 248. I am indebted to Dr. W. Muss-Arnolt for this reference. It was doubtless an Amorite word, and probably was not understood by the scribe, who living in Babylonia, where the surface of neglected fields turns white with salt, wrote the gloss "by night the fields became white."

[II šattu i-na ka-ša-di-šu] .... na-kan-t[um]	[When the second year arrives]....
[III šattu i-na] ka-ša-di	[When the third year] arrives,
[ni-šu i-na .... -ši-na] it-tak-ru	[The people in their]...became changed.
[IV šattu i-na ka-ša-di-šu ma-za-zi]-šu-nu ik-ru-ni	[When the fourth year arrives their position] is miserable.
[rap-ša-tu ....-ši-na] is-si-qa	[The wide .... their ....] became oppressed.
[qa-da-qad .... it-tal-la-ka ni-šu] i-na su-qi	[The people wander] in the street [with head bowed down].
[V šattu i-na ka-ša-di e-rib] ummi mârtu i-da-gal	[When the fifth year arrives], the daughter looks for [the entering] of the mother.
[ummu a-na mârti ul i-p]a-te bâbi-ša	[The mother op]ens not her door [to the daughter].
[zi-ba-ni-it ummi mârtu] i-na-ṭâl	[The daughter] looks upon [the treasures of the mother.]
[zi-ba-ni-it mârti i]-na-ṭal ummu	The mother looks upon [the treasures of the daughter.]
[VI šattu i-na ka-ša-di il-tak-nu] a-na nap-ta-ni mârta	[When the sixth year arrives, they prepare] the daughter for a meal.
[a-na pat-te bu-na] il-tak-nu	[For morsels] they prepare [the child].
[im-la-ni ma-šu .... bîtu i]l-ta-nu ša-nu-ú i-ri-ḫa-ma	[Full was ......] one house devours another.
[ki-i še-dim-me-te pa-nu-ši]-na kat-mu	[Like ghosts their faces] they cover.
[nišu i-na šu-par-ki]-e napišti bal-ṭa-at	[The people] live [in violence].
[bêl ta-ši-im-t]i A-tar-ḫasis amêlu	[The wise] Atra-ḫasis, the man,
[ana bêli-šu ᵈE]-a uzni-šú pi-ta-at	To E[a his lord], his thought turns.
[i-ta-m]u it-ti ili-šú	[He speaks] with his god.
[bêli-šu ᵈE-a] it-ti-šu la-šu i-ta-mu	[His lord Ea] speaks with him.
.... bâb ili-šú	.... the door of his god.
[i-n]a pu-ut nâri il-ta-kan ma-a-a-al-šú	By the river he places his bed.
.. me-iṭ-ra-tu-šú paq-rat	.... seek his rains.

B, II:56. Instead of *la-šu* Jensen read *la-a,* and considers it to be the negative particle. Dhorme also read it as the particle. Ungnad, and Rogers while regarding it as the negative, appreciated the difficulty added a question mark. It appears to be the Hebrew inseparable preposition with the pronominal suffix, which the scribe glossed with *it-ti-šu.*

B, II:59. *Me-iṭ-ra-tu-šu* has been translated "rains," see Dhorme. Jensen, Ungnad and Rogers do not translate. This is the Hebrew מָטָר in the plural, as recognized by Dhorme.

Column III.

.... *ir-ta*	....
[*eli*] *rig*(*ri-gi*)*-me-ši-na it-ta-d*[*ir*]	[Concerning] their cry he became troubled.
[*izzakar ina*] *ḫu-bu-ri-ši-na la i-ṣa-ba-ta* [*ni-ši-tu*]	[He spoke in] their assemblage to those untouched [by the desolations].
[*ᵈEn-l*]*il il-ta-kan pu-ḫur-*[*šu*]	[Enl]il held [his] assembly.
[*iz-za*]*-ka-ra a-na ilâni*^{meš} *marê*^{meš}*-šú*	[He sa]id to the gods his children,
[*iq*]*-tab-ta-ma* [*r*]*i-gi-im a-me-lu-te*	Those observing the clamor of men:
[*eli r*]*ig*(*ri-g*[*i*])*-me-*[*ši-n*]*a at-ta-a-*(*di-ir*)*dir*	[Concerning] their clamor I am troubled.
[*izzakar ina*] *ḫu-*[*bu*]*-ri-ši-na la i-ṣa-ba-ta ni-ši-tu*	[He said in] their assemblage to those untouched by the desolations.
.... *ma šu-ru-bu-u lib-ši*	........let there be malaria.
[*sur-r*]*iš li-ṣi ri-gim-ši-na nam-tar*	[Hast]ily let fate make an end to their clamor.
[*ki-m*]*a me-ḫi-e li-zi-qa-ši-na-ti-ma*	[Li]ke a storm, let it overwhelm them.
[*mur-ṣ*]*u ṭi-'u šú-ru-bu-u a-sa-ku*	[Sic]kness, headache, malaria, calamity.
.... *ma šú-ru-bu-u ib-ši*	...... and they had malaria.
[*sur*]*-riš*(*ri-iš*) *i-ṣi ri-gim-ši-na nam-tar*	[Hast]ily fate made an end to their cry.
[*ki-ma*] *me-ḫi-e i-zi-qa-ši-na-ti-ma*	[Like] a storm it overwhelmed them,
[*mur*]*-ṣu ṭi--'u šú-ru-bu-u a-sa-ku*	[Sick]ness, headache, malaria, calamity.
[*bêl ta*]*-ši-im-ti A-tar-ḫasis amêlu*	The wi[se lord] Atra-ḫasis, the man,
[*ana bêli*]*-šú ᵈE-a uzni-šu pi-ta-at*	To Ea, his [lord], his thought turns.
[*i-t*]*a-mu it-ti ili-šú*	[He sp]eaks with his god.
[*bêli*]*-šú ᵈE-a it-ti-šu i-ta-mu*	His [lord] Ea speaks with him.

B, III:3. The words here to be restored are probably *MU*(= *izzakar*) *a-na* (or *ina*), as in lines III:37, etc.

B, III:3. *La i-ṣa-ba-ta ni-ši-tu* was translated by Jensen "sollen nicht ...... erfassen;" by Dhorme "l'oubli ne l'atteindra pas;" by Ungnad "ergreift ihn nicht;" by Rogers "gives me no heed." The root of *i-ṣa-ba-ta* does not seem to be *ṣabâtu* "to take," but the well known Hebrew root עצב "to grieve, to be pained;" cf. עֲצוּבַת רוּחַ Is. 54:6, etc. This root was not current in Akkadian. The word *ni-ši-tu* which also occasioned difficulty, Dhorme has correctly compared with נְשִׁיָּה Ps. 88:13. This also is a Hebrew word.

B, III:4. Jensen has proposed that [*ᵈEn*]*-lil* be restored. Mr. Sidney Smith of the British Museum kindly informed the writer that the sign as reproduced in the text is correctly copied.

B, III:5. In the old version instead of *a-na ilâni mârê-šu* we have *e-na el*(?)*-li ra-bu-tim.*

A-tar-ḫasis pa-šu epuša(-ša) i-qab-bi	Atra-ḫasis opened his mouth, and speak
a-na ᵈE-a bêli-šú	To Ea, his lord.
bêlu ut-ta-za-ma ta-ni-še-ti	O lord, mankind is in misery.
lu-ku-nu-ma e-kal ma-tu	Your power consumes the land.
[*ᵈE*]*-a belu ut-ta-za-ma ta-ni-še-ti*	[E]a, O lord, mankind is in misery.
.... *ša ilâniᵐᵉˢ̌-ma e-kal ma-tu*	[The anger] of the gods consumes th land.
.... *ma te-ib-nu-na-ši-ma*	.... thou who hast created us
[*li-ip-par*]*-sa mur-ṣa ṭi-'u šú--bu-ru-u a-sa-ku*	Let sickness, headache, malaria, calamit ce[ase].
[*ᵈE-a pa-šu epuša(-ša) i*]*-qab-bi a-na A-tar-ḫasis me-izkur-šú*	[Ea opened his mouth], he speaks t Atar-ḫasis, and tells him:
...... *ka-lu-ša-pu-u i-na ma-ti*	.... in the land.
...... *-a tu-sa-pa-a ᵈIštar-ku-un*	.... pray to your goddess.
.... *-ka i-la par-ṣi-šú* 33 .... *tu niqu* 34 .... *ana qud-me-ša* 35 .... *-qat ra-ba-ma* 36 .... *nu-ka-at* ... [*il-ta*]*-kan(ka-an) qat-su*	.... god, his command.
[*En-lil.*]*il-ta-kan pu-ḫur-šú : izakkara a-na ilâniᵐᵉˢ̌ marêᵐᵉˢ̌-šú*	[Enlil] held his assembly; he speaks t the gods his children.
.... *ra me-e-ta aš-ku-na-ši-na-ti*	.... I will put them to death.
[*ṇišê*] *la im-ṭa-a a-na ša pa-na i-ta-at-ra*	[The people] have not become less; the are more numerous than before.
[*eli*] *rig-me-ši-na at-ta-a-dir*	[Concerning] their cry I am troubled.
[*izzakar ina*] *ḫu-bu-ri-ši-na la i-ṣa-ba-ta ni-ši-tu*	[He said in] their assemblage to thos untouched by the desolations.
[*lip-par*]*-sa-ma a-na ni-še-e ti-ta*	Let the fig tree for the people be [cu off].
[*i-n*]*a kar-ši-ši-na li-me-ṣu šam-mu*	[I]n their bellies let the plant be want ing.
[*e*]*-liš ᵈAdad zu-un-na-šú lu-ša-qir*	Above, let Adad make his rain scarce.

B, III:29. All the translations construe *me* as an emphatic particle. The writer regard it as the *waw consecutive*.

B, III:38. This has been read .... *ra-me e ta-aš-ku-na-ši-na-ti* "do nothing for them." *Me-e-ta* seems to be the Hebrew מָוֶת. However, as the passage is incomplete, this can onl be regarded as conjectural.

B, III:42. In the four transliterations the reading is given *ni-še e-ti-ta,* and is left untrans lated except by Dhorme, "aux gens la plante épineuse." See note under A, 9.

B, III:44. In the old version we have .... *šu ᵈAdad li-ša-aq-ṭi-il,* see A, 11. Probably Babylonian scribe did not know the Hebrew word, and changed the sense.

[li-is]-sa-kir šap-liš ia iš-ša-a me-lu i-na na-aq-bi	Below let (the fountain of the deep) be stopped, that the flood rise not at the source.
[l]i-šur eqlu iš-pi-ki-e-šú	Let the field withhold its fertility.
[l]i-ni-' irtu ša ^dNisaba : mušâti^meš lip-ṣu-u ugârê^meš	Let a change come over the bosom of Nisaba; by night let the fields become white.
ṣeru pal-ku-ú lu-li-id id-ra-nu	Let the wide field bear weeds(?).
[l]i-bal-kat ki-ri-im-ša : šam-mu ia ú-ṣa-a šu-ú ia i-'-ru	Let her bosom revolt, that the plant come not forth, that the sheep become not pregnant.
[li]š-ša-kin-ma a-na nišê^meš a-sa-ku	Let calamity be placed upon the people.
[rêmu] lu-ku-ṣur-ma ia ú-še-šir šir-ra	Let the [womb] be closed, that it bring forth no infant.
ip-[par-s]u a-na ni-šê-e ti-ta	The fig tree was cut [off] for the people.
i-na kar-ši-ši-na e-me-šu šam-mu	In their bellies, the plant was wanting.
e-liš ^dAdad zu-un-na-šú u-ša-qir	Above, Adad made scarce his rain.
is-sa-kir šap-liš ul iš-ša-a me-lu ina na-aq-bi	Below (the fountains of the deep) was stopped, that the flood rose not at the source.
iš-šur eqlu iš-pi-ki-šu	The field withheld its fertility.
i-ni-' irtu ša ^dNisaba : mušâti^meš ip-ṣu-u ugârê^meš	A change came over the bosom of Nisaba; the fields by night became white,
ṣeru pal-ku-ú ú-li-id id-ra-na : ib-bal-kat ki-ri-im-ša	The wide field bore weeds(?); her womb revolted.
šam-mu ul ú-ṣa-a šú-ú ul i'-ru	The plant came not forth; the sheep did not become pregnant.
iš-ša-kin-ma a-na nišê^meš a-sa-ku	Calamity was placed upon the people.
rêmu ku-ṣur-ma ul ú-še-šir šir-ra	The womb was closed, and brought forth no baby.

B, III:45. As already observed, A, 12 had been injured when the early text was written, and the subject of the verb was lost. It is also wanting in this text. We find the subject in Gen. 8:2, in the words "fountains of the deep." In Genesis the same form from the same verb is used, except that it is in the plural, namely יִסָּכְרוּ.

B, III:49. Jensen translated *šu-u ia i-'-ru* "Korn nicht ....ess!" Dhorme read *šu-u ia i-'-ru* "qu'elle ne germe pas!". Ungnad "Getride nicht kommen(?)!". Rogers, reading *šu-u i-im-ru,* translated "lambs shall not fatten." There are two occurrences of *šû* in the Annals of Sargon, see Delitzsch *HWB* 632. This also is the Hebrew word שֶׂה "one of a flock" (a sheep or a goat), here used collectively as in the O. T. The verb must be *i-'-ru* following B, III:59. This is the root הרה "to conceive."

COLUMN IV.

.... [^{d}]*E-a iz-za-kar*	...... Ea said.
...... *ú-šam(ša-am)-na-ši*	.... he shall cause her to recite.
.... [*tam*]-*nu ši-ip-ta : iš-tu-ma tam-nu-ú ši-pa-sa*	.... [reci]ted an incantation. After she recited the incantation;
[.... *i*]-*ta-di eli ṭi-iṭ-ti-ša*	[She sp]at upon her clay.
[*XIV gi-ir*]-*ṣi taq-ri-iṣ : VII gi-ir-ṣi ana imni taš-ku-un*	[Fourteen pieces] she pinched off; seven pieces she laid on the right.
[*VII gi*]-*ir-ṣi ana šumêli taš-ku-un : i-na be-ru-šu-nu i-ta-di libitta*	[Seven] pieces she laid on the left; between them she placed a brick.
.... *a ap-pa-ri pa-ri-iq a-bu-un-na-te tip-te-ši*	Offspring is delivered, the birth-stool(?).
[.... *is*]-*si-ma ir-še-te mu-te-ti*	She then called the wise ....
[*VII*] *u VII šà-su-ra-ti : VII u-ba-na-a zikarê*^{meš}	Seven and seven mothers, seven formed boys.
[*VII*] *ú-ba-na-a sinnišâti*^{meš}	Seven formed girls
[*š*]*à-su-ru ba-na-at ši-im-tu*	The mother, the creator of destiny.
ši-na-šan(ša-na) ú-ka-la-la-ši-na	Them(?), they finished them.
ši-na-šan(ša-na) ú-ka-la-la maḫ-ru-ša	Them(?), they finished before her.
ú-ṣu-ra-te ša nišê^{meš}*-ma ú-ṣa-ar* ^{d}*Ma-mi*	The figures of people, Mami formed.
i-na bît a-li-te ḫa-riš-ti : VII ûmê^{meš} *li-na-di libittu*	In the house of the bearing one the midwife, shall let the brick for seven days lie.
i-lut istu bît ^{d}*Maḫ e-riš-ta* ^{d}*Ma-mi*	Divinity(?) from the temple of Maḫ, the wise Mami,
šab-su-tu-um-ma ina bît ḫa-riš-ti li-iḫ-du	They that are angry in the house of the midwife, let be happy.
ak-ki a-li-it-tu u-la-du-ma	When the bearing one is about to give birth,
ummi šir-ri lu-ḫar-ri-ša ra-ma-an-[*ni-ša*]	Let the mother of the child conceive it like into herself.
[*zi*]-*ka-ru* .... 22 .... *el-li*	Male ....

C. ASSYRIAN FRAGMENT.[3]

....*lu-u*....)	....
....*ki-ma kip-pa-ti*	....like the ends of heaven,

[3] The text was published by Pinches IV R^2 Additions p. 9; and Delitzsch *Assyrische Lesestücke*[3] p. 101. It was translated by Haupt *KAT*[2] 61; Jensen *Kosmologie* 371f; *KB* VI 1 254f; Winckler *Textbuch* 94f; Jeremias *ATAO* 233; Dhorme *Choix* 126f; Ungnad *ATB* I 57; Rogers *Cuneiform Parallels* 104; and Jastrow *Heb. and Bab. Trad.* 344.

. . . . *lu-da-an e-liš u ša[p-liš]*	. . . . let it be strong above and below,
. . . . *e-pi-ḫi* . . . .)	. . . . . . close . . . . . .
. . . . *a-dan-na ša a-šap-pa-rak-[kum-ma]*	. . . . the time I will send thee.
[ana elippi] e-ru-um-ma bâb elippi tir-[ra]	. . . . enter and close the door of the ship.
. . . . . . *lib-bi-ša šeat-ka bušû-ka u makkuru-[ka]*	. . . . in it thy grain, thy possessions, and thy property,
[aššat]-ka ki-mat-ka sa-lat-ka u mârê^{meš} *um-ma-ni*	Thy [wife], thy family, thy relatives and the craftsmen,
bu-ul ṣêri u-ma-am ṣêri ma-la urqîti ir-	The cattle of the field, the beasts of the field, as many as dev[our] grass,
[a-šap-p]a-rak-kum-ma i-na-as-aṣ-ṣa-ru bâbi-[ka]	I will send thee, and they will guard thy door.
[At-ra]-ḫa-sis pa-a-šu epuš-ma iqabî	Atra-ḫasis opened his mouth, and spoke.
[iz-zak]-kar ana ^{d}*E-a be-li-[šu]*	He said to Ea, his lord:
ma-ti-ma-a elippi ul e-pu-uš	How long! I have not built a ship.
[ina qaq]-qa-ri e-ṣir u-[ṣur-tu]	Upon the earth draw a plan!
[u-ṣur]-tu lu-mur-ma elippu [lu-pu-uš]	The plan let me see, and I will build the ship.
. . . . *ina qaq-qa-ri e-ṣir*	. . . . upon the ground he drew.
. . . . *ša taq-ba-a*	. . . . . . which thou hast commanded.

D. A DELUGE STORY IN SUMERIAN.[4]

COLUMN III.

The beginning of the column is wanting.

ki- . . . . an-na? . . . . 11 uk[. . . . . 12 a-ma-ru . . . . 13 . . . . . . 14 . . . . -ne-ne in	The . . . . place . . . . 11 The people . . . . 12 The flood . . . . 13 . . . . 14 . . . . the made, ...
û-bi-a ^{d}Nin-t[u . . . . . .] dìm a-	At that time Nintu [cried aloud] like [a woman in travail].
azag ^{d}Innanna-gè uku-bi-šù a-nir mu-	The holy Ishtar lamented for her people. . . . .
^{d}En-ki šà-ní-te-na-gè ă-i-ni- . . . . -gí-gí	Ea in his own heart held counsel.

[4] The text, transliteration and translation were published by Poebel *Historical and Grammatical Texts* No. 1, and *Historical Texts* 14ff and 66ff. Translations are also found in Barton *Archaeology and the Bible* 280f; Jastrow *Heb. and Bab. Trad.* 335ff; and King *Legends of Babylon and Egypt* 62ff.

An ^{d}En-lîl ^{d}En-ki ^{d}Nin-ḫar-sag-gá-g[è]	Anu, Enlil, Ea and Nin-Ḫarsag ....
dingir-an-ki-gè mu An ^{d}En-líl mu-n[i]-....	The gods of heaven and earth inv[oked] the name of Anu (and) Enlil.
û-ba Zi-û-sùd-du lugal-ám pašiš	At that time Zi-û-sudda the king, the priest of ....
AN-SAG-gũr-gũr mu-un-dìm-dìm en	A great ...... he made ......
nam-BÚR-na KA-sí-sí-gi ní-te-gá	In humility he prostrates himself, in reverence ....
û-šu-uš-e sag-uš-gub-ba	Daily he stands in attendance ......
ma-mú-nu-me-a è-dé KA-bal	A dream, as had not been before, comes forth ......
mu--an-ki-bi-ta pá-pá-dé	By the name of heaven and earth he conjures. ....

Column IV.

[..]-..-šù dingir-ri-e-ne GIŠ ...	For ...... the gods. ....
Zi-û-sùd-du da. bi(?).gub-ba giš-mu..	Zi-û-suddu standing at its side heard ...
iz-zi-da á-gúb-bu-mu gub-ba	At the wall on my left side stand ......
iz-zi-da i(nim)-ga-ra-ab-dü-dü	At the wall I will speak a word to thee.
na-ri-ga-mu giš-TU-P[I]	My holy one, give attention!
šú-me-a a-ma-ru u-dü kab-d[ü-ga] ba-........	By our hand(?) a flood will be sent;
numun-nam-lù-qál ḫa-lam-e-d[é]	To destroy the seed of mankind ....
di-til-la i(nim)-pu-uḫ-ru-[um dingir-ri-e-ne-ka..]	Is the decision, the word of the assembly [of the gods]
dü-dü-ga An ^{d}En-[líl]	The commands of Anu (and) En[lil ...
[n]am-lugal-bi bal-bi	Its (their) kingdom, its (their) reign ..
e(?)-[n]e-šù	To him (them) ....
[.....]-na mu-	....

The rest of the column, or about three-fourths of the text, is missing.

Column V.

im-ḫul-im-ḫul-ní-gũr-gũr-gál dú-a-bi ur-bi ni-lăḫ-gi-eš	All the mighty windstorms together blew.
a-ma-ru u-dü kab-dü-ga ba-an-da-ab-ùr-ùr	The flood ...... raged.

D, IV:8. As Poebel has pointed out *pu-uḫ-ru-[um]* is Akkadian.

û-7-ám gê-7-ám	When for seven days, for seven nights
a-ma-ru kalam-ma ba-ùr-ra-ta	The flood overwhelmed the land.
^{gis}mà-gũr-gũr a-gal-la im-ḫul-bul-bul-a-ta	When the storm drove out the great boat over the mighty waters.
^{d}Utu i-im-ma-ra-è an-ki-a û-má-má	Shamash (the sun-god) came forth shedding light over the heaven and earth.
Zi-û-sùd-du ^{gis}mà-gũr-gũr KA(?)-BÚR mu-un-da-BÙR	Zi-û-suddu opened the [hatch] of the great boat.
šul-^{d}Utu giš-šír-ni(?).ša(?) ^{gis}ma-gũr-gũr-šù ba-an-tu-ri-en	The light of the hero Shamash enters into the interior(?) of the great boat.
Zi-û-sùd-du lugal-ám	Zi-û-suddu, the king,
igi-^{d}Utu-šù KA-ki-su-ub-ba-tûm	Prostrates himself before Shamash.
lugal-e gû im-ma-ab-gaz-e u[d]u im-ma-ab-šár-ri	The king sacrifices an ox; a sheep he slaughters(?).
....si-gal .... -la-da .... 13 .... mu-un-[n]a..... 14 ..... 15 ..... bí-in-si 16 .... tab-ba 17 .... a-[b]a	

The rest of the column is missing.

Column VI.

zi-an-na zi-ki-a ni-pá-dé-en-zi-en za-zu-da ḫe-im-da-lá	By the soul of heaven, by the soul of earth ye shall conjure him, That he may be .... with you.
An ^{d}En-líl zi-an-na zi-ki-a ni-pá-dé[-en]-ze-en za-da-ne-ne im-da-lá	Anu (and) Enlil by the soul of heaven, by the soul of earth shall ye conjure; He will be .... with you.
nig-gil-(ma) ki-ta é-dé im-ma-ra-é-dé	The *niggilma* of the ground rises in abundance.
Zi-û-sùd-du lugal-ám	Zi-û-suddu, the king,
igi An ^{d}En-líl-lá-šù KA-ki-su-ub-ba-tûm	Before Anu (and) Enlil prostrates himself
ti dingir-dìm mu-un-na-sí-mu	Life like (that of) a god he gives to him;
zi-da-rí dingir-dìm mu-un-na-ab-é-dé	An eternal soul like (that of) a god he creates for him.
û-ba Zi-û-sùd-du lugal-ám	At that time Zi-û-suddu, the king,
mu níg-gil-ma numun-nam-lù-qál-URU(?)-ag	The name of the *niggilma* (he named) "Presence of the seed of mankind"

kúr-bal kúr-dilmun(?)-na ki ....-šù mu-un-ti-eš	In a .... land, that of Dilmun, they caused him to dwell.
za- ....gal-bi(?)-ti(?)-eš-a	

The rest of the column, about three-fourths of the text, is missing.

.... -ra(?) Zi-û-sùd-du SAL ...

E. THE DELUGE STORY IN THE GILGAMESH EPIC.[5]

^{d}*Gilgameš a-na ša-šu-ma izakkara(-ra) a-na Ûm-napiš-tim ru-u-qi*	Gilgamesh said to him, to Ûm-napishtim, the distant one:
a-na-aṭ-ṭa-la-kum-ma Um-napiš-tim	I look upon thee, O, Ûm-napishtim;
mi-na-tu-ka ul ša-na-a ki-i ia-a-ti-ma at-ta	Thy appearance is not changed, for I am like thou art.
u at-ta ul ša-na-ta ki-i ia-ti-ma at-ta	And thou art not different, for I am like thou art.
gu-um-mur-ka lib-bi a-na e-piš tu-qu-un-ti	There is perfection of heart unto thee to make combat.
[*ina n*]*a-a-ḫi na-da-at-ta e-li(lu) ṣi-ri-ka*	And in resting thou liest upon thy back.
....*ki-i ta-az-ziz-ma ina puḫur ilâni*^{meš} *ba-la-ṭa taš-'-u*	[Tell me], how hast thou stood up, and found life in the assembly of the gods?
Ûm-napiš-tim ana ša-šu-ma izakkara (-ra) a-na ^{d}*Gilgameš*	Ûm-napishtim spoke to him, even to Gilgamesh;
lu-up-te-ka ^{d}*Gilgameš a-mat ni-ṣir-ti*	I will reveal, O Gilgamesh, the secret story;
u pi-riš-ta ša ilâni^{meš} *ka-a-ša lu-uq-bi-ka*	And the decision of the gods to thee I will relate.
^{âl}*Šu-ri-ip-pak ălu ša ti-du-šu at-ta*	Shurippak, a city which thou knowest,
[*ina a-ḫi*] ^{nar}*Pu-rat-ti šak-nu*	Is situated (on the bank) of the Euphrates,

[5] George Smith published the first translation in *The Chaldean Account of Genesis* 263ff (1876). The text is published in Delitzsch AL^3 101ff; Haupt *Nimrod-Epos* 133ff; and Pinches IV R^2 43f. Translations have been published also by Fox Talbot, Oppert, Lenormant, Haupt, Jensen, Jeremias, Winckler, Zimmern, King, Ball, Jastrow, Muss-Arnolt, Clay, Rogers, Barton and others. For comparative purposes the following four are freely quoted in the discussions in the notes: Jensen *KB* VI 1 228ff; Dhorme *Choix* 100ff; Ungnad *ATB* I 50ff; and Rogers *Cuneiform Parallels* 90ff.

E, 6. Instead of the usual reading [*u i-n*]*a a-ḫi na-da-at e-li ṣi-ri-ka* "thou liest down upon thy side, upon thy back" the writer proposes the above.

E, 9. The word *niṣirtu* meaning "hidden thing," as already noted, is Amorite.

âlu šu-u la-bir-ma ilâni^{meš} *kir-bu-šu*	That city was old when the gods within it,
[a-n]a ša-kan a-bu-bi ub-la lib-ba-šu-nu ilâni^{meš} *rabûte*^{meš}	The great gods, brought their hearts to send a deluge.
[kir]-ba-šu abu-šu-nu ^{d}*A-nu-um*	[These drew near] their father, Anu;
ma-lik-šu-nu qu-ra-du ^{d}*En-lil*	Their counselor, the warrior Enlil;
guzalû-šu-nu ^{d}*En-Urta*	Their herald, En-Urta;
gu-gal-la-šu-nu ^{d}*En-nu-gi*	Their hero, Ennugi.
^{d}*Nin-igi-azag* ^{d}*E-a it-ti-šu-nu ta-me-ma*	The lord of wisdom, Ea counseled with them; and
a-mat-su-nu u-ša-an-na-a a-na qi-ik-ki-šu	He repeated their words to the *qikkiš*:
qi-ik-kiš qi-ik-kiš i-gar i-gar	*Qikkiš, qikkiš!* Wall, wall!
qi-ik-ki-šu ši-me-ma i-ga-ru ḫi-is-sa-as	O, *qikkis*, hear! O wall, give attention!
amêl Šu-ru-up-pa-ku-u mâr Ubara-^{d}*Tu-Tu*	Man of Shurippak, son of Ubara-Tutu,
u-qur bîta bi-ni elippa	Tear down the house, build a ship!
muš-šir mešrê(-e) še-'-i napšâte^{meš}	Leave possessions, take thought for life!
na(?)-ak-ku-ra zi-ir-ma na-piš-ta bul-liṭ	Abandon property; save life!
[š]u-li-ma zêr nap-ša-a-ti ka-la-ma a-na lib-bi ^{iṣ}*elippi*	Bring into the ship the seed of life of everything!
^{iṣ}*elippu ša ta-ba-an-nu-ši at-ta*	The ship which thou shalt build,
l[u]-u man-du-da mi-na-tu-ša	Let its dimensions be measured!
[l]u-u mit-ḫur ru-bu-us-sa u mu-rak-ša	Let its breadth and its length be proportioned!
[ki]-ma ap-si-i ša-a-ši ṣu-ul-lil-ši	[Li]ke the *apsû*, protect it with a roof (*šâši*)!

E, 20. The writer feels that *qikkiš or qiqqiš* is an archaic Amorite word which is glossed by *igaru "wall."* A wooden wall would alone furnish material for the construction of the boat. *Ši-me-ma* is also apparently a gloss for *ḫi-is-sa-as*.

E, 26. If instead of *na-ak-ku-ra* the injured line should prove to read *ina ma-ak-ku-ra*, then *zi-ir-ma* would probably be from סור or זור "to turn aside", and the preceding line would be a gloss; the Akkadian word *i-zi-ir-an-ni* "hates me" occurs a few lines below.

E, 31. The word *ša-a-ši* also occurs in line 61, in *ša-a-ši e-ṣir-ši*. Jensen translates 31 "[B]eim Weltmeer leg es (, es) hin", Dhorme "Sur l'océan place-le!". Ungnad "[An] den Ozean lege es vor Anker(?)," Rogers ".... the heaven cover it with a roof," and Hilprecht "Cover it like the subterranean waters." Jensen translated line 60, "Ich warf hin die Vordergestalt zeichnete es;" Dhorme, "Je tracai ses contours, je les dessinai;" Ungnad, "Ich entwarf(?) den Vorderbau(?) und zeichnete es (das Schiff);" and Rogers, "I enclosed it."

The word *ša-a-ši* is perhaps to be identified with the Amorite form of Shamash, namely שוש see Clay *BE* X:116. Nabopolassar in a late building inscription from Sippar calls himself

[a]-na-ku i-di-ma a-zak-ka-ra a-na ^{d}*E-a be-li-ia*	I understood, and said to Ea, my lord,
....*-[u]r(?)be-li ša taq-ba-a at-ta ki-a-am*	[The word] of the lord, as thou hast commanded, thus
[at]-ta-'-id a-na-ku ep-pu-uš	I will observe, I will execute.
.... *[m]i(?) lu-pu-ul âlu um-ma-nu u ši-bu-tum*	[But what] shall I answer the city, the people, and the elders?
[^{d}*]E-a pa-a-šu i-pu-uš-ma i-qab-bi*	Ea opened his mouth and spoke.
i-zak-ka-ra ana ardi-šu ia-a-tu	He said unto me, his servant:
.... *lu at-ta ki-a-am ta-qab-ba-aš-šu-nu-ti*	Verily thou shalt say to them,
[a]-di-ma ia-a-ši ^{d}*Enlil i-zi-ir-an-ni-ma*	[I kn]ow that Enlil hates me, and
ul uš-šab ina a[li-ku]-nu-ma	I may not dwell in your city;
[in]a qaq-qar ^{d}*En-lil ul a-šak-ka-[na] pâni-ia-a-ma*	Nor on the soil of Enlil set my face.
[ur]-rad-ma ana apsî it-ti ^{d}*[E-a be]-li-ia aš-ba-ku*	I will go down to the ocean; with [Ea] my lord, I will dwell.
[eli k]a-a-šu-nu u-ša-az-na-an-ku-nu-ši nu-uḫ-šam-ma	[Upon] you will he (Enlil) then rain abundance.
[bu-'-ur] iṣṣure^{meš} *bu-[']-ur nûnê*^{meš} *ma*	[A catch of] birds; a catch of fish,
.... *[ra-b]a-a e-bu-ra-am-ma*	.... a harvest, and
.... *[mu-ir] ku-uk-ki (ina li-la-a-ti)*	.... When the *muir kukki*, in the evening,
[u-ša-az-na-nu-ku]-nu-ši ša-mu-tum ki-ba-a-ti	Will send you a heavy rain.
[mim-mu-u še-e-ri] ina na-ma-a-ri	...... glows
.... *[a]š-ma-a* ... 50 ... *pa-as(z, ṣ) u* ... 51 *[k]a(?)* ... 54 *u* ... *pi* .... ta	...... heard ....

About fifty lines missing.

šir-ru ...... *[iš]-ši kup-ra*	.... bore the asphalt.
dan-nu ina .... *[ḫi]-šiḫ-tu ub-la*	Strong .... I brought the neces[sities].

mi-gi-ir ^{d}*Ša-aš-šu KB* III 2, 8:10. It is written without the determinative *KB* III 64:11, 13. The word seems to mean Shamash, as hitherto noted. In the deluge text above, does it not refer to the course through which Shamash travels, namely the firmament, the covering, the vault above the earth? The word *apsû* was a synonym. The passage it would seem should be translated, "like the *apsû*, enclose it with a roof". In the case of the deluge ship, it was absolutely necessary that it have a roof.

ina ḫa-an-ši û-mi [a]t-ta-di bu-na-ša	On the fifth day, I raised its form.
aš-kan ḫi-sa 10 *GAR*$^{\text{ta-a-an}}$ *šaq-qa-a igârâti*^{meš}*-ša*	I placed its walls about its perimeter 120 cubits high.
10 *GAR*$^{\text{ta-a-an}}$ *im-ta-ḫir ki-bir muḫ-ḫi-ša*	120 cubits was proportioned the length of its upper part.
ad-di la-an-ši ša-a-ši e-ṣir-ši	I laid its hull; I enclosed it with a roof (*šâši*).
ur-tag-gi-ib-ši a-na VI-šu	I covered it (i. e. made decks) six times.
ap-ta-ra-as [pa-ri-s]u a-na VII-šu	I divided (into divisions) seven times.
qir-bi-is-zu ap-ta-ra-as a-na IX-šu	I divided its interior nine times.
^{iṣ}*sikkâti mê ina qabli-ša lu-[u] am-ḫas-si*	Water-tanks in its midst I constructed.
a-mur pa-ri-su u ḫi-šiḫ-tum ad-di	I inspected the compartments, and I installed the necessities.
VI šar ku-up-ri at-ta-bak a-na qi-i-ri	Three sars of bitumen I smeared over the (outside) wall.
III šar iddî [at-ta-bak] a-na lib-bi	Three sars of bitumen I smeared over the inside.
III šar ṣabê^{meš} *na-aš* ^{iṣ}*su-us-su-ul-ša i-zab-bi-lu šamna*	Three sars of oil the basket bearers brought in.
e-zi-ib (e-zu-ub) šar šamni ša i-ku-lu ni-iq-qu	I saved a sar of oil which sacrifices consumed.
II šar šam-[ni] u-pa-az-zi-ru ^{amêl}*malâḫu*	Two sars of oil the shipman stowed away.
a-na n[išê^{meš}*] uṭ-ṭib-bi-ih alpe*^{meš}	For [the people] oxen were slaughtered.

E, 58. Jensen read *ina KAN-ḪI-SA* "nach dem plan;" Dhorme, *ina KAN ḫi-sa* "Quant a son enceinte;" Ungnad, "Nach dem Entwurf(?)"; Rogers *ina KAN-sa sa* "in its plan." The sentence preceding and the eight that follow all contain a verbal form, which, with the exception of line 59, are in the first person singular. The writer proposes the above reading. If it is correct, *aš-kan* may be a dialectical form of *aš-kun*.

E, 60. Jensen translated *la-an* "Vordergestadt", Dhorme "contours;" Ungnad, "Vorderbau;" and Rogers, "hull." It seems to the writer that the word does refer to the hull or bottom, and that the root is very probably the Hebrew לון "to lodge, pass the night;" because that is the part of the boat in which the people lodged.

E, 66. The word *ki-i-ri* is translated by Jensen "Innenraum;" Dhorme "l' interieur;" Ungnad "den Schmelzofen(?)" and Rogers "outside(?)." As already noted, *qîru* is the Hebrew קיר "wall."

E, 68. *Su-us-su-ul-lu* is (Jensen *KB* VI 1 p 490) Amorite; cf. סלסלות Jer. 6:9..

E, 70. The root of *u-pa-az-zi-ru* is the common Hebrew בצר "to gather, gather in, enclose." While the word *puzru* "concealment," and *pazru*, "concealed" in Akkadian may be from the same root, the verb with the above meaning was not in current use.

aš-gi-iš immêrê^meš^ u-mi-šam-ma	I slew sheep daily.
si-ri-[šu ku-ru]-un-nu šamnu u karanu	Must, sesame wine, oil and wine.
um-ma-[na aš-qi] ki-ma me nâri-ma	I gave the workmen to drink like water from the river.
i-sin-[na aš-ku-na] ki-ma û-mi a-ki-tim-ma	[I made a fe]ast like the Akitu festival, and
ap-t[e] ... piš-ša-ti qa-ti ad-di	I open[ed a box] of ointment. I completed my task (lit. laid down my hand).
l[a-a]m ^d^Šamaš ra-bi-e elippu gam-rat	Before(?) Shamash, the great ship was finished.
.... *šup-šu-qu-ma*	.... was opened wide, and
gi-ṣa(?) elippa epušu^meš^ uš-tab-bi-lu e-liš u šap-liš	The ship ropes(?) which they made, they installed above and below.
.... *li-ku-ši-ni pat-su*	...... their ...... were ......
[mimma i-šu-u e]-ṣi-en-ši	With all that I had, I loaded it.
mimma i-šu-u e-ṣi-en-ši kaspu	With all that I had of silver, I loaded it.
mimma i-[šu-u e]-ṣi-en-ši-en-ši ḫurâṣu	With all that I had of gold, I loaded it.
mimma i-šu-[u e-ṣi-en]-ši zêr napšâte^meš^ ka-la-ma	With all the seed of life that there was, I loaded it.
uš-te-li a-[na] libbi elippi ka-la kim-ti-ia u sa-lat-ia	I caused to go up into the ship all my family and relatives.
bu-ul ṣeri u-ma-am ṣeri mârê^meš^ um-ma-a-ni ka-li-šu-nu u-še-li	The cattle of the field, the beast of the plain, the craftsmen, all of them, I caused to go up.
a-dan-na ^d^Šamaš iš-ku-nam-ma	Shamash fixed a time (saying),
mu-ir ku-uk-ki ina li-la-a-ti u-ša-az-na-an-nu ša-mu-tu ki-ba-a-ti	The *muir kukki* at even will send a heavy rain.
e-ru-ub ana [lib]-bi elippi-ma pi-ḫi bâb (elippa)-ka	Enter the ship and close the door.
a-dan-nu šu-u ik-tal-da	That time arrived.
mu-ir ku-[uk-ki] ina li-la-a-ti i-za-an-na-nu ša-mu-tu ki-ba-a-ti	The *muir kukki* at even sent a heavy rain.
ša û-mi at-ta-ṭal bu-na-šu	Of the storm, I observed its appearance.
û-mu a-na i-tap-lu-si pu-luḫ-ta i-ši	To behold the storm, I dreaded.
e-ru-ub a-na lib-bi elippi-ma ap-te-ḫi ba-a-bi	I entered the ship, and closed the door.

E, 76. In all the translations *qa-ti ad-di* is made to refer to the "ointment." It seems to the writer that it is an expression meaning, he finished the task.

E, 81. On *e-ṣi-en-ši* from the Amorite root עצן ; see Chap. I.

a-na pi-ḫi-i ša elippi a-na Bu-zu-ur-^{d}Amurru ^{amêl}malâḫi	To the master of the ship, to Buzur-Amurru, the sailor,
ekallu at-ta-[di-i]n a-di bu-še-e-šu	I entrusted the great house, including its possessions.
mim-mu-u še-e-ri ina na-ma-ri	On the appearance of the break of dawn,
i-lam-ma iš-tu i-šid šamê^{meš} ur-pa-tum ṣa-lim-tum	There rises from the foundation of the heavens a black cloud.
^{d}Adad ina lib-bi-ša ir-tam-ma-am-ma	Adad thunders in the midst of it.
^{d}Nabû u ^{d}Šarru il-la-ku ina maḫ-ri	Nebo and Sharru go before.
il-la-ku guzalê^{meš} šadu-u u ma-a-tum	They go as messengers over mountain and land.
tar-kul-li ^{d}Ura-gal i(u)-na-as-saḫ	Urragal tears out the mast(?).
il-lak ^{d}En-Urta mi-iḫ-ra u-šar-di	En-Urta proceeds; he advances the onset.
^{d}A-nun-na-ki iš-šu-u di-pa-ra-a-ti	The Anunnaki raise the torches.
ina nam-ri-ir-ri-šu-nu u-ḫa-am-ma-ṭu ma-a-tum	With their flashes they illuminate the land.
ša ^{d}Adad šu-mur-ra-as-[su] i-ba-'-u šamê(-e)	The fury of Adad reaches the heavens.
[mim]-ma nam-ru ana e-[ṭu-ti] ut-tir-ru	Everything that was bright turns [to darkness].
.... *mâtu kima e* .... *iḫ-še(b[u])-*	...... the land; like ......
išten(-en) û-ma me-	One day, the deluge.
ḫa-an-tiṣ i-zi-qam-ma .... *mat-a*	Quickly it overwhelms, and [covers] the mountains.
ki-ma qab-li eli [nišê^{meš} u-ba]-'-u	Like a war engine it comes upon the people.
ul im-mar a-ḫu a-ḫa-šu	Brother could not see brother.
ul u-ta-ad-da-a niše^{meš} ina šamê(-e)	The people in heaven did not recognize each other.
ilâni^{meš} ip-la(tal)-ḫu a-bu-ba-am-ma	The gods fear the deluge.
it-te-iḫ-su i-te-lu-u ana šamê(-e) ša ^{d}A-nim	They withdraw, they ascend to the heaven of Anu.
ilâni^{meš} kima kalbi kun-nu-nu ina ka-ma-a-ti rab-ṣu	The gods cower like a dog; they lie down in the enclosure.
i-šes-si ^{d}Iš-tar ki-ma a-lit-ti	Ishtar cries like a woman in travail.

E, 95. The word *pi-ḫi-i* is not Akkadian, but it is the Hebrew פֶּחָה; and it seems that to regard the latter as borrowed from the Babylonian *piḫâtu* "district," as is generally done, is a mistake.

u-nam-ba ^{d}be-lit i[lâni] ṭa-bat rig-ma	The lady of the gods wails with her beau tiful voice.
u-mu ul-lu-u a-na ṭi-iṭ-ṭi lu-u i-tur-ma	The former day is verily turned to clay
aš-šu a-na-ku ina pu-ḫur(ma-ḫar) ilâni^{meš} aq-bu-u limutta	When I spoke evil in the assembly of th gods—
ki-i aq-bi ina pu-ḫur(ma-ḫar) ilâni^{meš} limutta	O, that I spoke evil in the assembly o the gods,—
ana ḫul-lu-uq niše^{meš}-ia qab-la aq-bi-ma	For the destruction of my people, I or dered the cataclysm.
a-na-ku-um-ma ul-la-da ni-šu-u-a-a-ma	I verily will bear (again) my peopl (which)
ki-i mârê^{me} nûnê^{meš} u-ma-al-la-a tam-ta-am-ma	Like a spawn of fish fill the sea.
ilâni^{meš} šu-ut ^{d}A-nun-na-ki ba-ku-u it-ti-ša	The gods of Anunnaki weep with her.
ilâni^{meš} aš-ru aš-bi i-na bi-ki-ti	The gods are depressed; they sit weep ing;
kat-ma(šab-ba) šap-ta-šu-nu [pa-ah-ra]-a pu-uḫ-ri-e-ti	Their lips are silent; [they huddle together.
VI ur-ri u mu-ša-a-ti	Six days and six nights,
il-lak ša-a-ru a-bu-[bu me]-ḫu-u i-sap-pan mâtu	The wind tears, and the deluge-tempes overwhelms the land.
si-bu-u û-mu i-na ka-ša-a-di it-ta-rak (v. rik) me-ḫu-u a-bu-bu qab- la	When the seventh day arrives, the de uge-tempest subsides in the onslaugh
ša im-daḫ-ṣu ki-ma ḫa-ai-al-ti	Which had fought like an army.
i-nu-uḫ tâmtu uš-ḫa-ri-ir-ma im-ḫul-lu a-bu-bu ik-lu	The sea rested; the hurricane had sper itself, the flood was at an end.
ap-pa-al-sa-am-ma û-ma(ta-ma-ta) ša-kin qu-lu	I looked upon the sea; the voice wa silent.
u kul-lat te-ni-še-e-ti i-tu-ra a-na ṭi-iṭ-ṭi	And all mankind was turned to clay.
ki-ma u-ri mit-ḫu-rat u-sal-lu	Like a log they floated about.
ap-ti nap-pa-ša-am-ma urru im-ta-qut eli dûr ap-pi-ia	I opened the hatch, and the light fe upon my countenance.
uq-tam-mi-iṣ-ma at-ta-šab a-bak-ki	I was horrified, and I sat down and wep

E, 131. As already mentioned, *ḫa-aja-al-ti* is Hebrew; see Jensen *KB* VI 1 p. 498.

E, 133. In the duplicate text *ta-ma-ta* takes the place of *û-mu*, showing that the latt should not be translated "day," as is done by all translators, but "sea" (= ים).

eli dûr ap-pi-ia il-la-ka di-ma-a-a	Over my countenance ran my tears.
ap-pa-li-is kib-ra-a-ti ḫat-tu tâmti	I looked in all directions; the sea was terrible.
a-na XII$^{\text{ta-a-an}}$ *i-te-la-a na-gu-u*	On the twelfth day, an island arose.
a-na ^{šad}*Ni-ṣir i-te-mid* ^{iṣ}*elippu*	Upon Mount Niṣir, the ship grounded.
šadû(-u) ^{šad}*Ni-ṣir elippa iṣ-bat-ma a-na na-a-ši ul id-din*	Mount Niṣir held the ship that it moved not.
isten(-en) u-ma šana-a û-ma šadû(-u) Ni-ṣir Ki-Min	One day, a second day, Mount Niṣir held it, that it moved not.
šal-ša û-ma ri-ba-a û-ma šadû(-u) Ni-ṣir Ki-Mín	A third day, a fourth day Mount Niṣir held it, that it moved not.
ḫan-šu šiš-ša šadû(-u) Ni-ṣir Ki-Min	A fifth day, a sixth day Mount Niṣir held it, that it moved not.
siba-a û-ma i-na ka-ša-a-di	When the seventh day arrived,
u-še-ṣi-ma summata^{iṣṣur} *u-maš-šir*	I brought out and released a dove.
il-lik summatu^{iṣṣur} *i-tu-ra-am-ma*	The dove went forth; it turned;
man-za-zu ul i-pa-aš-šum(šim)-ma is-saḫ-ra	It did not have a resting place; it returned.
u-še-ṣi-ma sinûndu^{iṣṣur} *u-maš-šir*	I brought out and released a swallow.
il-lik sinûndu^{iṣṣur} *i-tu-ra-am-ma*	The swallow went forth; it turned;
man-za-zu ul i-pa-aš-šum-ma is-saḫ-ra	It did not have a resting place; it returned.
u-še-ṣi-ma a-ri-ba u-maš-šir	I brought out and released a raven.
il-lik a-ri-bi-ma qa-ru-ra ša mê i-mur-ma	The raven went forth; it saw the drying up of the water;
ik-kal i-ša-aḫ-hi i-tar-ri ul is-saḫ-ra	It approached; it waded; it croaked(?); it did not return.
u-še-ṣi-ma a-na IV šârê at-ta-qi ni-qa-a	I sent (everything) to the four winds. I offered a sacrifice.
aš-kun sur-qi-nu ina eli ziq-qur-rat šadî(-í)	I made a libation upon the summit of the mountain.
VII u VII ^{karpat}*a-da-guru uk-tin*	Seven and seven *adagur* pots I set out.

E, 137. Jensen translates "kniete neider;" Dhorme, "Je m'affalai;" Ungnad, "Ich kniete hin;" Rogers "I bowed." It seems to the writer that the root of *uq-ta-am-mi-iṣ* may possibly be the Hebrew קוץ to feel a loathing, abhorrence;" cf. line 126.

E, 142. Poebel (*ibid.* p. 55) has already pointed out that the root of *na-a-ši* is not *nâšu* "to sway, quake, tremble." As it is a synonym of *alâku* 2 R 35:50 e f, it seems to the writer that the root is the Hebrew נוס "to escape," cf. Is. 59:19. Professor Torrey has kindly called my attention to the *haf'el* of this verb meaning "remove" in the two old Aramaic inscriptions, namely the Zakir II:20, and the Nerab Inscription I:6, and II:8, 9; see *JAOS* 35, 363; and *AJSL* 33, 54 f.

i-na šap-li-šu-nu at-ta-bak qanâ ^{giš}erina u âsa	Beneath them I piled reeds, cedar woo and myrtle.
ilâni^{meš} i-ṣi-nu i-ri-ša	The gods smelled the savor.
ilâni^{meš} i-ṣi-nu e(i)-ri-ša ṭa-[a-ba]	The gods smelled the sweet savor.
ilâni^{meš} ki-ma zu-um-be-e eli bêl niqê ip-taḫ-ru	The gods like flies gathered about th sacrificer.
ul-tu ul-la-nu-um-ma ^{d}bêlit ilâni ina ka-ša-di-šu	When finally the lady of the gods a rived.
iš-ši NIM^{meš} rabûte^{meš} ša ^{d}A-nu-um i-pu-šu ki-i ṣu-ḫi-šu	She raised the great jewel(?), whic Anu had made according to her wish.
ilâni^{meš} an-nu-ti lu-u ^{abnu}ṣibri-ia ai am-ši	Ye gods here, I shall not forget my necl lace.
ûmê^{meš} an-nu-ti lu-u aḫ-su-sa-am-ma ana da-riš ai am-ši	Upon these days I shall think, so th forever I will not forget.
ilâni^{meš} lil-li-ku-ni a-na sur-qi-ni	Let the gods come to the offering.
^{d}En-lil ai il-li-ka a-na sur-qi-ni	Enlil shall not come to the offering;
aš-šu la im-tal-ku-ma iš-ku-nu a-bu-bu	Because he took not counsel; and sent tl deluge;
u nišê^{meš}-ia im-nu-u a-na ka-ra-ši	And my people he numbered for destru tion.
ul-tu ul-la-nu-um-ma ^{d}En-lil ina ka-ša-di-šu	When at last Enlil arrived,
i-mur elippa-ma i-te-ziz ^{d}En-lil	He saw the ship; then Enlil was wroth
lib-ba-ti im-ta-li ša ilâni^{meš} ^{d}Igigi	He was filled with anger against tl Igigi gods.
ai-um-ma u-ṣi na-piš-ti	Has anyone come out alive?
ai ib-luṭ amêlu ina ka-ra-ši	No man shall survive the cataclysm.
^{d}Enurta pa-a-šu epuš-ma iqabbi	En-Urta opened his mouth, and spake,
izakkar(-ar) ana qu-ra-di ^{d}En-lil	He said to the warrior Enlil;
man-nu-um-ma ša la ^{d}E-a a-ma-ti i-ban-[nu]	Who without Ea shall devise the con mand?
u ^{d}E-a i-di-e-ma ka-la šip-ri	And Ea knows every matter.
^{d}E-a pa-a-šu epuš-ma iqabbi	Ea opened his mouth and spoke,
izakkar(-ar) ana qu-ra-di ^{d}En-lil	He said to the warrior Enlil:
at-ta abkal ilâni^{meš} qu-ra-du	Thou wise one(?) of the gods, O wa rior,
ki-i ki-i la tam-ta-lik-ma a-bu-ba taš-kun	Why, O why hast thou not taken counse and hast sent a flood?
be-el ḫi-ṭi (ar-ni) e-mid ḫi-ṭa-a-šu	On the sinner place his sin;
be-el ḫab-la-ti e-mid ḫab-lat-su	On the evil doer place his crimes;

ru-um-me ai ib-ba-ti-iq šu-du-ud ai . . .	That charity (?) be not cut off; that punishment be not . . . .
am-ma-ki taš-ku-nu a-bu-ba	Instead of thy sending a deluge,
nêšu lit-ba-am-ma nišê^{meš} *li-ṣa-aḫ-ḫi-[ir]*	Let a lion come and diminish the people.
am-ma-ki taš-ku-nu a-bu-ba	Instead of thy sending a deluge,
barbaru lit-ba-am-ma nišê^{meš} *li-ṣa-a[ḫ-ḫi-ir]*	Let a wolf come and diminish the people.
am-ma-ki taš-ku-nu a-bu-ba	Instead of thy sending a deluge,
ḫu-šaḫ-ḫu liš-ša-kin-ma mâtu liš-[giš]	Let there be a famine and ruin the land.
am-ma-ki taš-ku-nu a-bu-ba	Instead of thy sending a deluge,
^{d}*Ur-ra lit-ba-am-ma mâtu (nišê*^{meš}*) liš-giš*	Let Urra come and destroy the people.
a-na-ku ul ap-ta-a pi-riš-ti ilâni^{meš} *rabûte*^{meš}	I have not revealed the decision of the great gods.
At-ra-ḫa-sis šu-na-ta u-šab-ri-šum-ma pi-riš-ti ilâni^{meš} *iš-me*	I caused Atra-ḫasis to see a dream, and he heard the decision of the gods.
e-nin-na-ma mi-lik-šu mil-ku	Now take counsel concerning him.
i-lam-ma ^{d}*Ea a-na lib-bi elippi*	Ea went up into the ship.
iṣ-bat qa-ti-ia-ma ul-te-la-an-ni-ia-a-ši	He took my hand, and brought me up.
uš-te-li uš-ta-ak-mi-is sin-niš-ti ina i-di-ia	My wife he brought up, (and) caused to kneel beside me.
il-pu-ut pu-ut-ni-ma iz-za-az ina bi-ri-in-ni i-kar-ra-ban-na-ši	He turned our faces and he stood between us; he blessed us.
i-na pa-ni Ûm-napištim a-me-lu-tum-ma	Formerly Ûm-napishtim was a man, and
e-nin-na-ma Ûm-napištim u sinništi-šu lu-u e-mu-u ki-i (ma) ilâni^{meš} *na-ši-ma*	now Ûm-napishtim and his wife are associates; they are elevated like gods.
lu-u a-šib-ma Ûm-napištim ina ru-u-qi ina pi-i nârâti^{meš}	Verily Ûm-napishtim shall dwell afar off at the mouth of the rivers.
il-qu-in-ni-ma ina ru-qi ina pi-i nârâti^{meš} *uš-te-ši-bu-in-ni*	He took me, and caused me to dwell afar off at the mouth of the rivers.

F. A FRAGMENT OF DELUGE STORY IN BABYLONIAN.[6]

. . . . *ša (?) ša (?) . . . . . . -ka*	. . . .
. . . . *a-pa-aš-šar-[ma]*	. . . . I will loosen;
. . . . . . *ka-la ni-ši iš-te-niš i-za-bat*	. . . . . . will take all the people together.

[6] Published by Hilprecht *BE* Ser. D V 1 33f. It was also translated by Rogers *Cuneiform Parallels* 108f; and by Jastrow *Heb. and Bab. Trad.* 343f.

...... *-ti la-am a-bu-bu wa-ṣi-e*	...... before the deluge comes;
.... *-a-ni ma-la i-ba-aš-šu-u lu--kin ub-bu-ku lu pu-ut-tu ḫu-ru-šu*	...... as many as there are I will bring destruction. Verily observe silence.
...... ^{is}*elippa ra-be-tam bi-ni-ma*	...... build a great ship; and
.... *ga-be-e gab-bi lu bi-nu-uz-za*	...... the total height, shall be its structure.
...... *ši-i lu* ^{is}*magurgurrum ma-šum-ša lu-na-ṣi-rat na-piš-tim*	...... It(she) shall be a *magurgurrum* (giant boat); and her name shall be 'the reserver of life.'
.... *ri(?) zu-lu-la dan-na zu-ul-lil*	...... protect with a great cover.
.... *te-ip-pu-šu*	...... which thou shalt make.
.... *u-ma-am ṣi-rim iṣ-ṣur ša-me-e*	...... beast of the field, fowl of the heaven.
.... *ku-um mi-ni*	...... for a number (or of a kind).
.... *u qi[n]-ta*	...... and family. ....

G. BEROSSUS' VERSION OF THE ATRA-ḪASIS EPIC.[7]

After the death of Ardatos, his son Xisouthros reigned for eighteen sars; in his reign a great deluge took place, and the story has been recorded as follows.

Kronos appeared to him in his sleep and said that on the fifteenth of the month Daisios men would be destroyed by a deluge. He bade him therefore, setting down in writing the beginning, middle, and end of all things, to bury them in Sippara, the city of the Sun; to build a boat, and go aboard it with his family and close friends; to stow in it food and drink, to put in it also living creatures, winged and four-footed, and when all his preparations were complete, to set sail; when asked where he was sailing, to say, "To the gods, in order to pray that men may have blessings."[8] He did not disobey, but built the[9] boat, five[10] furlongs

F, 5. The root of *ḫu-ru-šu* seems to be the Hebrew חרש "to be silent, speechless."

F, 7. It has been shown that גבה is the root of *ga-be-e* (see Hilprecht, *BE* Ser. D V p. 51).

F, 8. Poebel anticipated the writer in the rejection of the reading *ba-bil* (see *Historical Texts* p. 61); however, the *ma* which follows is not an emphatic particle, but the Hebrew *waw conjunctive.*

F, 9. Rogers correctly translated; "with a strong roof cover it."

[7] The text followed is that of A. Schoene *Eusebi Chronicorum Libri Duo* Vol. I pp. 20-24, except where differences are noted. The translation and notes here presented are by my colleague, Prof. A. M. Harmon of Yale University.

[8] Through ambiguity caused by indirect discourse, the Greek might almost equally well mean: "When asked (by Xisouthros) where he was to sail, he (Kronos) said" etc. It was so taken by the author of the Armenian version.

[9] *ναυπηγῆσαι τὸ* A. M. H., *ναυπηγήσαντα* Ms, *ναυπηγήσασθαι* Gutschmid.

[10] Gutschmid and Schoene follow the Armenian version, "fifteen."

in length and two furlongs in width, assembled and stowed everything in accordance with the directions, and embarked his wife and children and his close friends.

After the deluge had begun and had quickly ceased, Xisouthros let some of the birds go; but as they found no food nor place to alight, they came back into the boat. Again after some days Xisouthros let the birds go, and they came back to the boat with their feet muddy. But when they were let go for the third time, they did not come back to the boat again. Xisouthros concluded that land had appeared; unstopping some part of the boat's seams and perceiving that the boat had grounded upon a mountain, he disembarked with his wife, his daughter, and the helmsman; and after he had done homage to the earth, built an altar, and sacrificed to the gods, disappeared with all those who had disembarked from the boat. Those who had remained in the boat disembarked when Xisouthros and his companions failed to come in, and looked for him, calling him by name. Xisouthros himself they never saw again, but a voice came from the air, telling them that they must be pious, for because of his piety he was gone to live with the gods; and that his wife, his daughter, and the helmsman had received a share in the same honor. He told them, too, that they would go back to Babylonia, and that it was fated for them to recover the writings at Sippara and publish them to men; also that the country where they were belonged to Armenia. On hearing this, they sacrificed to the gods and went by a roundabout way[11] to Babylonia. But of this boat that grounded in Armenia some part still remains there, in the mountains of the Kordyaioi in Armenia, and people get pitch from the boat by scraping it off, and use it for amulets.

They went, then, to Babylonia, dug up the writings at Sippara, founded many cities, built temples, and so repopulated Babylonia.

[11] *πέριξ* Ms, *πεζῇ* Schoene.

DYNASTIC LISTS OF EARLY BABYLONIA.[12]

I Kish Kingdom

4	.... -um-e	
5	.... -an-	
6	.... -vu-um	
7	[Uph-] ba(?)	
8	.... tabba	
9	Kalumum	900 yrs.
10	Zugagib	840 "
11	Arwû, s. of a *mushkenu*	720 "
12	Etana, the Shepherd	625 "
13	Baliqam, s.	410 "
14	En-men-nun-na	611 "
15	Melam-Kish	900 "
16	Bar-sal-nun-na, s.	1,200 "
17	Mes-za-mug(?), s.	
18	En-gis(?)-gu(?), s. of No. 16	
19	En-me-dur-mes-e(?)	
20	.... -za	
21	En-me-bara-gi-šu(?)	
22	....	900 "
23	Ag(?), s. of En(?)	625 "
	23 kings	18,000 + x

Eanna or I Uruk Kingdom

1	Mesh-kin-gasher, s. of Shamash	325 yrs.
2	En-mer-kár, s.	420 "
3	Lugal Marda, the Shepherd	1,200 "
4	Tammuz, the Hunter	100 "
5	Gilgamesh, s. of High-priest of Kullab	126 "
6	...-lugal, s.	
	11(?) kings (about 5 missing)	2,171 + x

I Ur Kingdom

1	Mesh-anni-pada	80 yrs.
2	Mesh-kiag-nunna, s.	30 "
3	Elulu	25 "
4	Balulu	36 "
	4 kings	171 "

Awan Kingdom

	3 kings	356 yrs.

II Kish Kingdom

	Mesilim	
	Al-zu(?)	
	Ur-sag-e	
	4(?) kings	3,792 yrs.

Ḫamazi Kingdom

1	...-ni-ish	7 years

I Adab Kingdom

	Lugal-dalu	
	Me-igi-...	
	2(?) kings	

II Ur Kingdom

	Annani	
	Lu-Nannar, s.	
	4(?) kings	108 yrs.

II Adab Kingdom

	Lugal-anni-mundu	
	1 king	90 yrs.

Mari Kingdom

	Ansir	30 "
	...-gi	
	I-[sh]ar-Shamash	
		30+ yrs.
	3(?) kings	

I(?) Akshak Kingdom

1	Zuzu	

[12] The dynastic lists published by the writer in *JAOS* 41 244ff. are here reproduced with some modifications and additions based on a few additional finds published by Legrain *Historical Fragments* 10ff.

III Kish Kingdom

1 Eannatum
Lugal-tarsi
3 Enbi-Ashtar

3(?) kings

II Uruk Kingdom

Enshagkushanna
Lugal-kigub-nidudu
Lugal-kisalsi

3(?) kings

II(?) Akshak Kingdom[13]

1	Un-zi	30 years	3077?
2	Un-da-lu-lu	12 "	3047?
3	Ur-sag	6 "	3035?
4	BÁ-ŠA-Saḫan	20 "	3029?
5	Ishu-il	34 "	3009?
6	Gimil-Sin, s.	7 "	2985?
	6 kings	99 years	

IV Kish Kingdom

1	Azag-Bau or Bau-ellit	14 years	2978?
2	BÁ-ŠA-Sin, s.	25 "	2964?
3	Ur-^{d}Zababa	6 "	2939?
4	Zimutar	30 "	2933?
5	Uzi-watar, s.	6 "	2903?
6	El-muti	11 "	2897?
7	Imu-Shamash	11 "	2886?
8	Nania, the Jeweler	3 "	2875?
	8 kings	106 years	

III Uruk Kingdom

1	Lugal-zaggisi, s. of Ukush	25 years	2872?

Akkad Kingdom

1	Sharru-kin	55 years	2847?
2	Uru-mush, s.	15 "	2792?
3	Manishtusu, s.	7 "	2777?
4	Naram-Sin, s.	56 "	2770?
5	Shargali-sharri, s.	25 "	2714?
6	*Manum šarru manum la šarru*		
7	Igigi		
8	Imi		
9	Nanum	3 "	2689?
10	Ilulu		
11	Dudu	21 "	2686?
12	Su-qar-kib, s.	15 "	2665?
	12 kings	197 years	

IV Uruk Kingdom

1	Ur-nigin	3 years	2650?
2	Ur-gigir, s.	6 "	2647?
3	Kudda	6 "	2641?
4	BÁ-ŠA-ili	5 "	2635?
5	Ur-Shamash	6 "	2630?
	5 kings	26 years	

Gutium Kingdom

1	Imbia	5 years	2624?
2	Ingishu	7 "	2619?
3	Warlagaba	6 "	2612?
4	Iarlagarum	3? "	2606?
8	[ ]-gub		
9	[ ]-ti		
10	[ ]-an-gub		
11	[ ]-bi		
	Arlagan		
	E-ir-ri-du-pi-zi-ir		
	Šarlak		

[13] The dates from Utu-ḫegal backward are uncertain, because the 25 years assigned that ruler are conjectural and also because it is not known whether any other kings intervened between his time and the reign of Ur-Engur of Ur. The date 2193 B. C., usually accepted for the beginning of Hammurabi's reign, is used as a starting point.

	Las-si-ra-ab		
	Si-ù-um		
21	Tirigan		
	21 kings	125 years	

V Uruk Kingdom

1	Utu-ḫegal	25? years	2499?

III Ur Kingdom

1	Ur-Engur	18	years	2474
2	Dungi, s.	58	"	2456
3	Amar-Sin, s.	9	"	2398
4	Gimil-Sin, s.	7	"	2389
5	Ibi-Sin, s.	25	"	2382
	5 kings	117	years	

Nîsin Kingdom			Larsa Kingdom		Babylon Kingdom		
B.C.		years		years		years	B.C.
2357	Ishbi-Urra	32	Naplanum	25			
2325	Gimil-ilishu, s.	10	Emiṣu	28			
2315	Idin-Dagan, s.	21	Samûm	35			
2294	Ishme-Dagan, s.	20	Zabaia	9			
2274	Libit-Ishtar	11	Gungunu	27			
2263	Ur-Enurta	28	Abi-sarê	11			
2235	Bur-Sin, s.	21	Sumu-ilu	29	Sumu-abum	14	2225
2214	Iter-pîsha, s.	5	Ǹûr-Immer	16	Sumu-la-ilum	36	2211
2209	Urra-imitti	7	Sin-idinnam	7?			
2202	Sin(?)-	½	Sin-iribam	2			
2201	Ellil-bâni	24	Sin-iqîsham	6			
2177	Zambia	3	Ṣili-Immer	1	Zabium	14	2175
2174	....	5	Warad-Sin	12			
2169	Ea....	4			Abil-Sin	18	2161
2165	Sin-mâgir	11					
2154	Dâmiq-ilishu, s.	23	Rim-Sin	61			
					Sin-muballiṭ	20	2143
	Years	225½	Ḫammurabi	12	Ḫammurabi	43	2123

THE SITE OF NISIN

The site of Nisin, which has previously been sought for in vain, is very probably at last located. A little over two years ago cones of Libit-Ishtar were brought to Baghdad and offered to the writer for purchase. It seemed that the provenance of these cones would determine the site of the city. Recently Captain Bertram S. Thomas kindly informed the writer, in a letter dated March 22d, that Col. Kenlys L. Stevenson had found a cone at Bahriyat, about seventeen miles south of Nippur. The mounds are simply a series of the usual "mud pie variety," as the English officers describe them. Bahriyat, it would seem, is the sought-for site.

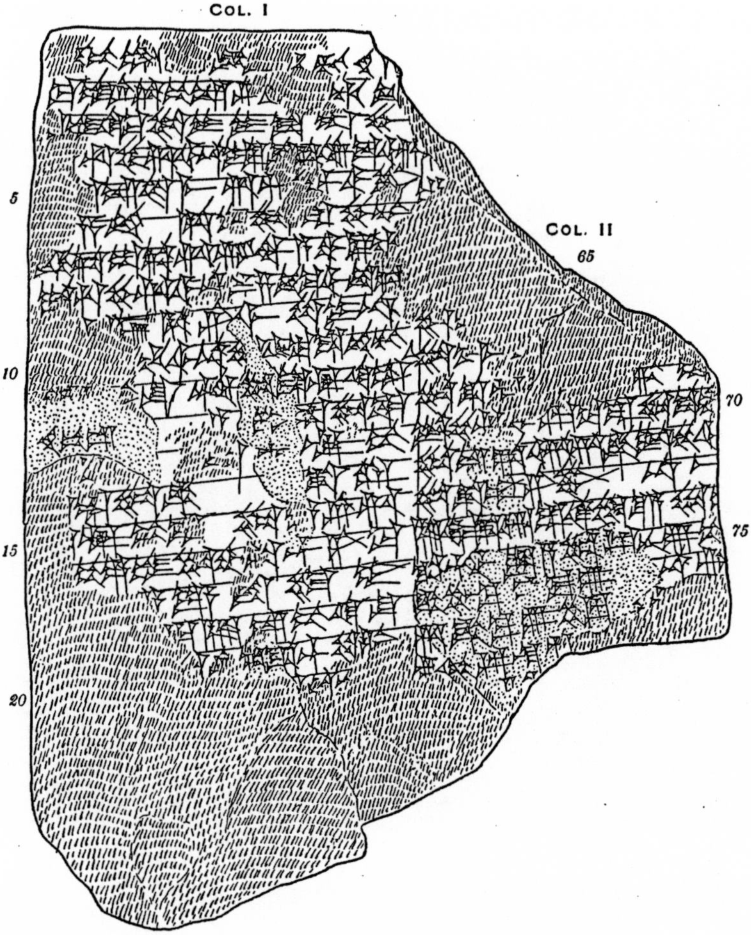

EARLY VERSION OF THE ATRA-HASIS EPIC
A HEBREW DELUGE STORY IN CUNEIFORM (OBVERSE)

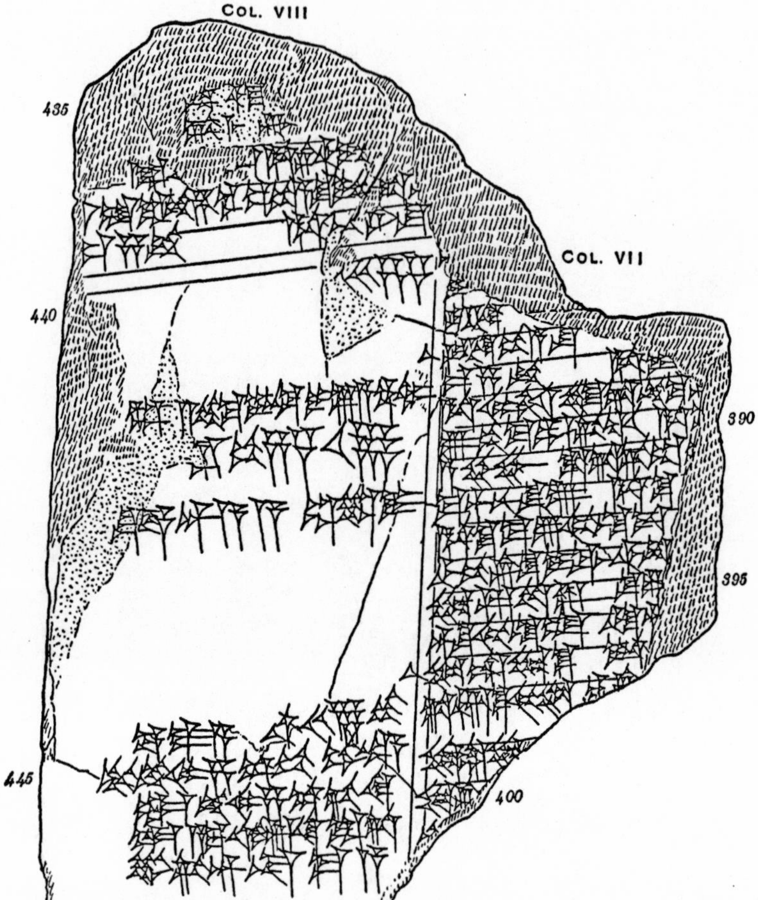

A HEBREW DELUGE STORY IN CUNEIFORM (REVERSE)

COL. I

COL. II

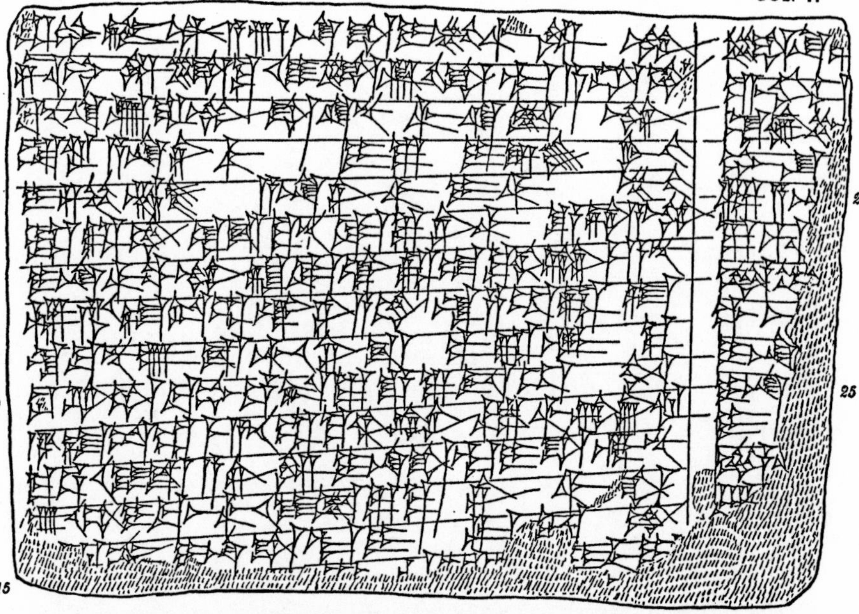

COL. VI

COL. V

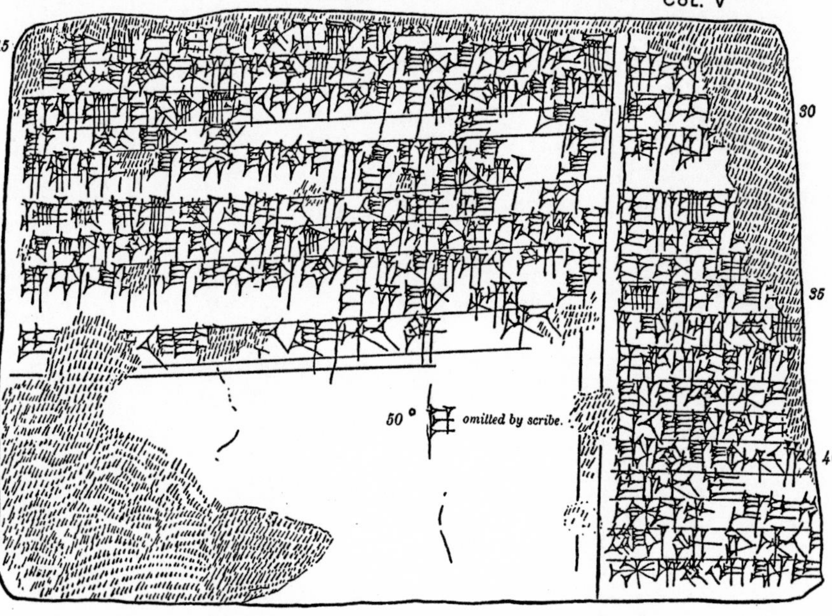

ANCIENT VERSION OF THE ETANA LEGEND

3

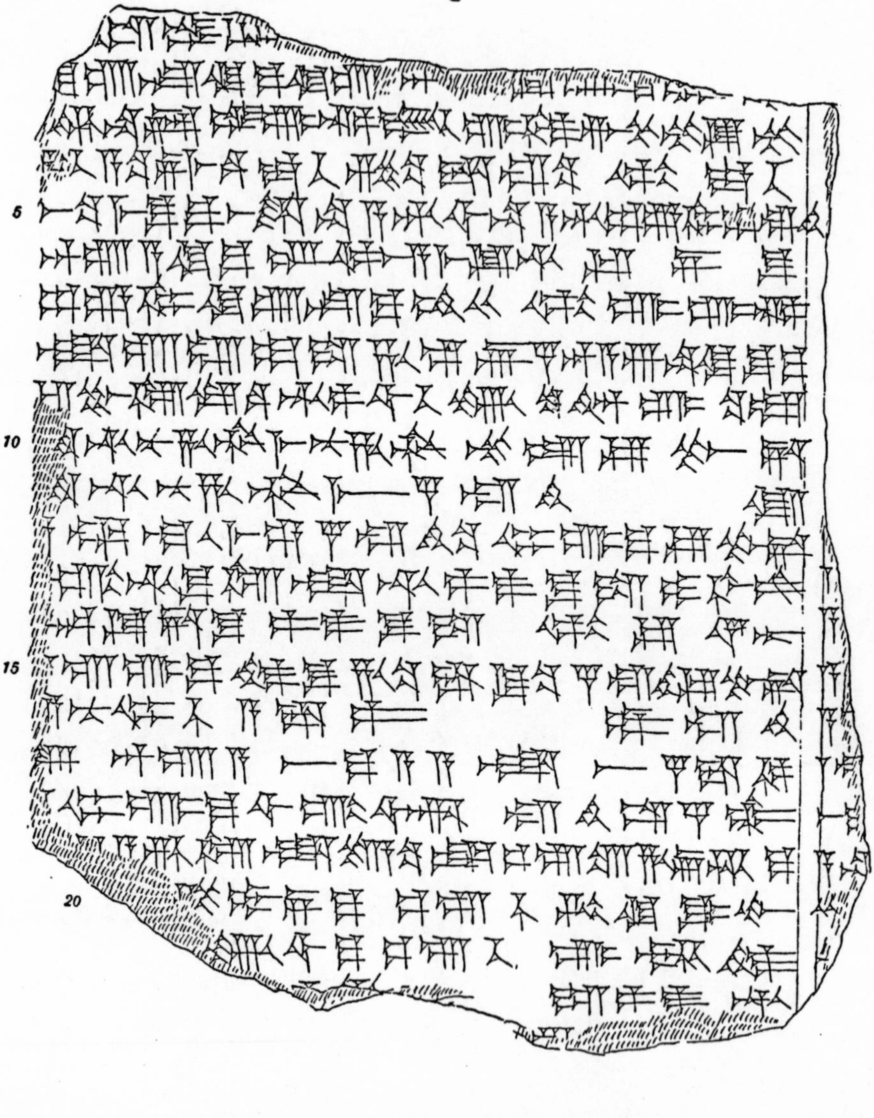

THE ADAPA LEGEND (OBVERSE)

A HEBREW DELUGE STORY IN CUNEIFORM (OBVERSE)
(SIZE OF ORIGINAL)

PLATE VI

A HEBREW DELUGE STORY IN CUNEIFORM (REVERSE)
THE ADAPA LEGEND (REVERSE IS DESTROYED)
(SIZE OF ORIGINALS)

ANCIENT VERSION OF THE ETANA LEGEND
(SIZE OF ORIGINAL)

THE ORIGINS OF DRAGON MYTHOLOGY

Paul Tice

Dragon slaying goes to the very root of humanity. There is virtually no culture the world without the dragon in its myth or folklore. The dragon could well be e most widespread symbol known to man. But what does it *mean,* and where did is symbol originate?

The most familiar place for us to look in the Western world is in the Bible. ere, combat with the dragon most always signifies the primordial struggle tween the forces of order and of chaos. Later, in the prophetic sense, it refers to e end of the world battle where Satan, the dragon, falls. But this is not where the mbol began. Other older cultures must be considered.

The theme is found in India when Indra slays Vritra. The Roman St. Sylvester lls a dragon. The Hebrew Daniel destroys Bel, the Greek Hercules kills Hydra, e Babylonian Marduk triumphs over Tiamat, the Egyptian sun gods battle pophis, Ahura Mazda slays Azhi Dahaka in Iran. In Japan the storm god, Susa- -wo, rescues a princess by chopping a dragon to pieces. Dragon slaying is also ferred to in *The Iliad*, by Homer.

The Middle ages and later give us dragon slayers in stories of the heroic St. eorge, Tristram, Siegfried, and King Arthur. And today, in modern Europe, an nual pageant recreates the slaying of dragons.

The theme is so powerful that it has followed us throughout history. Why? fter all, no physical evidence for dragons has ever been found – no bones, fossils, *thing*. Yet people throughout the world all seem to "remember" them. What is ing on here?

A possible answer exists if we accept that we may have inherited some sort of odly blood," or cosmic memory, from the gods themselves – gods who original- dealt with dragons in early myths. I could divert into support for this theory, but is argued more convincingly by such esteemed researchers as Zecharia Sitchin, eil Freer, Lee and Vivian Gladden, Christian O'Brien, John Cohane, Max Flindt d Otto Binder, only to name a few.

Evidence for alien or godly "blood" can also be found in the Bible. If *Genesis* read carefully, one will notice two distinct and separate "creations." The second these "creations" is the one falling under modern-day scrutiny. It is being close- examined in relation to the origins of us – modern *Homo Sapiens* – and points t a possible genetic connection to the gods. This connection is documented in ligious stories, literature, and myths worldwide.

The point is, if we *are* related to the gods in such a way, we humans may have tendency to "recall" similar myths (collectively speaking), including ones of agons – even if we've never seen a real dragon. This includes primitive, isolated

Dragon Slaying: The oldest and most common myth in the world.

cultures that had many common myths between them, but no means of travel spread such tales throughout the world.

To understand the dragon's origin clearly, we must start from the most bas concepts found in each myth:

The myths of dragon slaying follow a particular pattern. Dragons are usual found near water. That is its element – it represents both water and darkness. T dragon is causing trouble somewhere so a hero steps forward in an effort to slay

The hero is sometimes a god of light or a sun god. If he happens to be huma he's a representative of truth or light. It seems unlikely the hero will win, but does – with the help of a secret weapon or special powers. He's then worshipped becomes famous for the deed.

But where can we find the original pattern for this myth? What started t story? Where was the *first* dragon and who was the hero who slew it? The answers may be traced to the gods, *real* gods who were here on earth and foug with "dragons," as opposed to being mere "stories."

Many references about such gods point to the Babylonian creation myth call *Enuma Elish*. It means "When Above," and tells the story of the gods before the arrival on Earth. After their arrival we have the Old Testament, which states th "there were giants in the earth in those days . . ." Yet, the original Hebrew wo *Nefilim* translates *not* to the word "giants," but to "those who came down."

When we examine the *Enuma Elish* and *Genesis* together, we find no inconsi tencies and can actually see them overlap in a shockingly similar story. Anoth source for *Genesis* was the *Atra-Hasis*, already covered by Barranger in the prev ous chapter.

The *Enuma Elish* epic was translated from 7 clay tablets uncovered by vario archaeologists between the years 1848-1929 (part of the 5th tablet is still missi today). These discoveries were made in what was once called Mesopotamia – t cradle of civilization. The table have received a great deal of atte tion from scholars worldwide f many reasons. To start, the strongly resemble the first 2 cha ters of Genesis from the O Testament, but were written lo before it. Reading both provides more complete and interesti story of our forgotten past.

A Babylonian depiction of Tiamat.

Secondly, the story offe clues about the creation of the un verse and our solar system, inclu ing the earth itself. It is within th creation story, but closer to t end, that we find our first "dra on."

To understand the first dra on, we must briefly tell this cr ation story, the *Enuma Elish*. begins with "the divine parent and their offspring. All that exis is Apsu – the male creative go Tiamat, mother Earth (or the go dess of creation), and Mumm their son.

These male and female genders are probably just "terms" more than actual gen-rs. The only known Babylonian depiction of the monster Tiamat is included here. shows "her" with an unmistakable male appendage. This is interesting. We find e same thing in ancient Egypt, where the Earth is not female as we accept it today, it the sky is female, instead. She is Nuit and her male counterpart, Geb, is the irth. Gender is important only insofar as it provides a context for the interaction opposing or differing forces.

The *Enuma Elish* reveals Tiamat as the primeval saltwater ocean – possibly a assive, early version of planet Earth before some kind of catastrophe. She is a atery chaos, not being "formed" in the way we know now.

From here, scholarly interpretations vary but each leads to the appearance of ir dragon. By comparing any existing interpretation with any other we can see w elusive myth can be (as there will be differences). Yet, between these views we ay still sense an element of truth that has somehow been retained – as is often said out myths. Two of the more interesting views of the epic are those of Alexander eidel and Zecharia Sitchin. They have their differences, as noted above, so to oid confusion I will focus primarily on one.

Alexander Heidel's interpretation is found in his book called *The Babylonian enesis* and is worth looking into, however, I will focus on Zecharia Sitchin's.

Sitchin, in his books *The 12th Planet* and *Genesis Revisited*, interprets Apsu, e primary god, as the Sun. He attributes this to Sumerian texts, where the word inslates into "One Who Exists From the Beginning." Sitchin also tells us Mummu as the planet Mercury – "One Who Was Born," and that Tiamat was an earlier irth. With Sitchin, the Sun, Earth, and Mercury are followed by the births of the maining planets, although the exact process isn't revealed.

The epic continues, revealing that various generations of gods and goddesses e born. This could refer to the creation of additional planets or to beings who pear and start moving the planets around (much scientific and observable evi-nce exists for early cataclysmic events in the solar system). The universe comes active with much noise from the young gods. It disturbs Apsu and Tiamat ie sun and Earth) greatly, for their peaceful existence is lost.

Apsu and Mummu come to Tiamat with a plan to quiet things once and for all. iey will slay the young gods. Tiamat objects to destroying their own creations, but psu insists on doing it.

When the young gods hear the news they panic and run about aimlessly. They ially calm down and realize something must be done to save themselves. One of e young gods, Ea, casts a spell of sleep over Apsu to the point of his "death," and bs him of some important power he holds. This takes the most powerful entity out the picture and puts a halt to the plan of destroying the young gods. The usurp-Ea and his wife then give birth to Marduk – who will appear later as the first agon slayer.

Tiamat is greatly distressed at the loss of her creator-god husband. Apsu was so the father and respected leader to many loyal gods. After his "death," some of e gods get wicked ideas. Led by Kingu, they go to Tiamat and convince her to enge her husband's death. She could be next, being an equally powerful partner. id if someone killed or disabled *your* husband, who's job was to provide justice, ouldn't you then seek out that justice with the help of friends? They plan for bat-. During the plan, Tiamat creates 11 different kinds of monsters to help them. ie or more is a dragon:

With poison instead of blood she filled their bodies.

Ferocious dragons she clothed with terror,

She crowned them with fear inspiring glory and made them like gods.

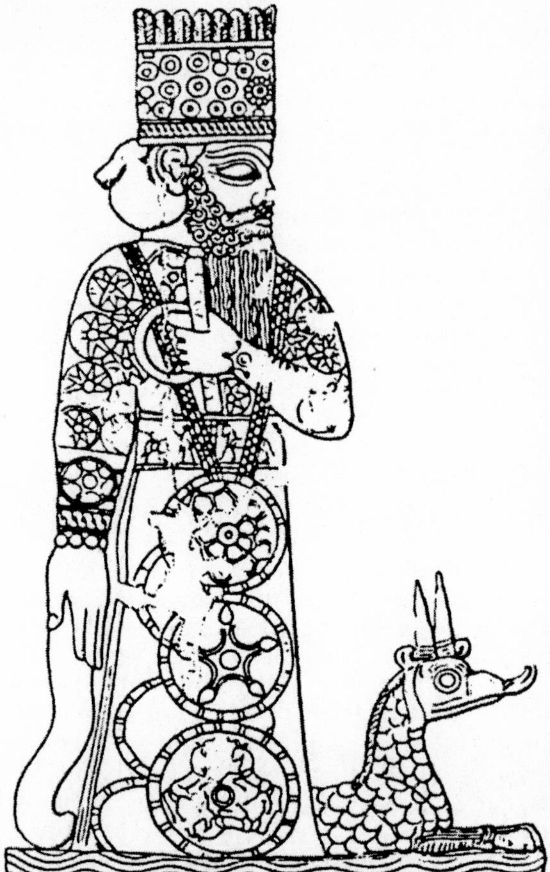

Marduk and the dragon.

But they are up again Marduk – the new warrior go These dragons fight bravely wi Tiamat against Marduk but a defeated with her. Marduk ki her with a powerful wind a piercing arrow. He then splits h huge corpse in two, creatir "heaven" and "earth" from t separate parts. All the rebel go are taken captive and enslave The story continues into oth areas, leaving the dragon behin

Most references state th Tiamat herself was the drag (and a male). This is not so. At point in the original epic is it sta ed. In a tablet uncovered Ashur, providing a similar ve sion of the story, *the dragon also clearly masculine* whi Tiamat is feminine. She was goddess of creation who ma these 11 monsters, including t dragon. The dragon was *creat* by her. As a result, later stor tellers of the *Enuma Elish* m have found the dragon ima helpful for listeners to visuali the events surrounding Tiam For example, the epic tells ho Tiamat opened her mouth in effort to devour Marduk – b failed.

Sitchin states that Tiamat, at least half her body, is now the "earth" we stand on. The "heaven" part of Tiam could well be the fragments in the asteroid belt, as he also explains.

Where is the dragon today? Myths throughout history most always place it water. We find mythical "sea monsters" dating back to the early sea-farers, goi up to present-day sightings of the Loch Ness Monster and a host of other likenes es. The dragon seems to have survived the battle, hiding deep within the confin of its mother. And with all of our mythologies there seems to be some kind "hero" lingering within us, that still wants to slay it.

So where do we find a dragon in order to accomplish this? In Loch Ness? N There is still no physical evidence. We are still searching for it, and it reflects in o beliefs. Down through our entire history, all heroic action seems to mimic th dragon myth. Many human actions mimic other myths as well. The best and mo respected scholars in the field of mythology have stressed this fact, includi Joseph Campbell. There seems to be an "archetypal blueprint" functioning in t background of our lives, and we unknowingly (for the most part) follow it. How d this come to be? Genetics might play a role. Some unknown genetic factor or advanced but unconscious ability to tap into a mythologically-based "collecti unconscious" (shared with the gods), could be involved.

The second creation of mankind (when godly genetic material was introduc to us) gave us a godly inheritance that allows us to "remember" dragons. Yet it w

Tiamat as "the dragon," attempting to devour Marduk.

›ne for the purpose of creating a worker, a "lullu," to help the gods. We not only :lped them, but worshipped them. Neil Freer mentions in *Breaking The Godspell* at the original meaning of the word "worship" meant "to work for." We did both.

Early man had to be made smart enough to work for the gods, including min-g their precious minerals, but stupid enough not to rebel (as the godly workers emselves had done).

Upon reflection, what do we see today? Any changes?? Many grudgingly ıdge off to jobs they dislike every day, wondering if there is some better way to ve. We were not only "created" to work, but programmed for it.

During this process of creating a modern worker, did the gods of old genetically ıss on to us some kind of hidden "memories"? It seems the answer is "yes," and e archetypes are at work within us. Including dragons. This is why we can't find real "dragon" or dig up any bones.

The scholarly pundits of the day brush this off and tell us the dragon is simply product of mythology and the human mind . . . The human mind? They mean the ›nscious part – that we made it up. But we don't know what 88% of the human ind is doing! We use only about 12% of it, and I must reiterate that archetypes are ›t conscious.

Dragons are our most powerful motif, something all cultures share through ory and myth. This powerful, pervasive archetype makes it impossible for us to ıow exactly what the first dragon really was. There are no absolutes in myth. [yths are about gods and take place, for the most part, with little human involve-ent.

Gods are known to be from another realm, a realm which undoubtedly lacks ıysical proof as we know it. Champ, Ogopogo, and The Loch Ness Monster ould all attest to this. Without physical proof, dragons are accepted as "imag-ed." Yet we've *seen* these things! Somewhere in the back of our minds lies the ıe answer.

Let's examine this. How do we actually view or perceive the dragon? What ›es it represent to us? The mind conjures up a depiction of evil – dragons are ways mean, and are the enemy. Tiamat was a goddess of watery depths that were :ep and dark (from here sprang the dragon); Marduk was a god of light, from ›ove instead of below.

We associate darkness with evil, but darkness is just darkness. It is *we* who ıve made it evil. Like the Chinese yin and yang, there is a balance within us that essential for our existence. One part is below the surface – our subconscious – ıd is shrouded in darkness. It is the home of our deepest mysteries, including the agon. We fear it, so have labeled it "evil." Abraham Maslow once said, "above l, we fear the godlike in ourselves."

The dragon, hidden below the Earth's surface in its watery element. Occasional "sightings" have occurred throughout history.

The other half is t conscious mind that v understand more clear and are therefore mo comfortable with. Ma of us mistakenly belie that the conscious mind all there is, and is clever responsible for our drag stories. Not so. Myths a dragons are residents the unconscious, a seem to fascinate us all.

Even if the drag surfaces in our conscio minds only on occasion, still has a reality of own. It is a deeper, hidd reality. A memory. A archetype. And an inhe tance.

Memories of the dra on have been passed on us in a way we don't ful comprehend, only to be accessed today through imaginative tales. The hum imagination keeps the dragon alive.

Einstein once said "Imagination is more important than knowledge." It cou be so. We do not *know* that dragons exist, but we imagine them. We should nev forget that the mind is very powerful, and to the human imagination, all things a real.

REFERENCES AND RECOMMENDED READING

1) King, L.W., *Enuma Elish: The Seven Tablets of Creation*, Book Tree, 199

2) Freer, Neil, *Breaking The Godspell*, Book Tree, San Diego, CA, 2000.

3) Heidel, Alexander, *The Babylonian Genesis*, University of Chicago Pres 1963.

4) Hogarth, Peter, *Dragons*, Viking Press, New York, N.Y., 1979.

5) Holiday, F.W., *Creatures From The Inner Sphere* (formerly titled *T Dragon And The Disc*), Popular Library, New York, N.Y., 1973.

4) Huxley, Francis, *The Dragon*, Thames & Hudson, New York, N.Y., 1989.

7) Neumann, Erich, *The Origins And History Of Consciousness*, Princet University Press, 1973.

8) Sheperd, Paul, *Nature And Madness*, Sierra Club Books, San Francisco, C 1982.

9) Sitchin, Zecharia, *The 12th Planet*, Avon Books, New York, N.Y., 1978.

10) Sitchin, Zecharia, *Genesis Revisited*, Avon Books, New York, N.Y., 199

This slightly revised text appears as part of a larger work titled *Mysteri Explored: The Search for Human Origins, UFOs and Religious Beginnings*, b Jack Barranger and Paul Tice, published by The Book Tree, 2000. ISBN 1-5850 101-4.

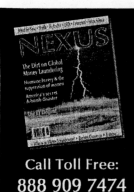

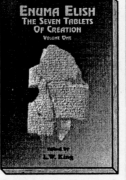

Of Heaven and Earth: Essays Presented at the First Sitchin Studies Day, edited by Zechar Sitchin. ISBN 1-885395-17-5 • 164 pages • 5 1/2 x 8 1/2 • trade paper • illustrated • $14.95

God Games: What Do You Do Forever?, by Neil Freer. ISBN 1-885395-39-6 • 312 pages • 6 9 • trade paper • $19.95

Space Travelers and the Genesis of the Human Form: Evidence of Intelligent Contact in tl Solar System, by Joan d'Arc. ISBN 1-58509-127-8 • 208 pages • 6 x 9 • trade paper • illustrated $18.95

Humanity's Extraterrestrial Origins: ET Influences on Humankind's Biological ar Cultural Evolution, by Dr. Arthur David Horn with Lynette Mallory-Horn. ISBN 3-931652-31 • 373 pages • 6 x 9 • trade paper • $17.00

Past Shock: The Origin of Religion and Its Impact on the Human Soul, by Jack Barrangı ISBN 1-885395-08-6 • 126 pages • 6 x 9 • trade paper • illustrated • $12.95

Flying Serpents and Dragons: The Story of Mankind's Reptilian Past, by R.A. Boulay. ISB 1-885395-38-8 • 276 pages • 6 x 9 • trade paper • illustrated • $19.95

Triumph of the Human Spirit: The Greatest Achievements of the Human Soul and How I Power Can Change Your Life, by Paul Tice. ISBN 1-885395-57-4 • 295 pages • 6 x 9 • tra paper • illustrated • $19.95

Mysteries Explored: The Search for Human Origins, UFOs, and Religious Beginnings, Jack Barranger and Paul Tice. ISBN 1-58509-101-4 • 104 pages • 6 x 9 • trade paper • $12.95

Mushrooms and Mankind: The Impact of Mushrooms on Human Consciousness ar Religion, by James Arthur. ISBN 1-58509-151-0 • 103 pages • 6 x 9 • trade paper • $12.95

Vril or Vital Magnetism, with an Introduction by Paul Tice. ISBN 1-58509-030-1 • 124 pages 5 1/2 x 8 1/2 • trade paper • $12.95

The Odic Force: Letters on Od and Magnetism, by Karl von Reichenbach. ISBN 1-58509-00 8 • 192 pages • 6 x 9 • trade paper • $15.95

The New Revelation: The Coming of a New Spiritual Paradigm, by Arthur Conan Doyle. ISB 1-58509-220-7 • 124 pages • 6 x 9 • trade paper • $12.95

The Astral World: Its Scenes, Dwellers, and Phenomena, by Swami Panchadasi. ISBN 58509-071-9 • 104 pages • 6 x 9 • trade paper • $11.95

Reason and Belief: The Impact of Scientific Discovery on Religious and Spiritual Faith, Sir Oliver Lodge. ISBN 1-58509-226-6 • 180 pages • 6 x 9 • trade paper • $17.95

William Blake: A Biography, by Basil De Selincourt. ISBN 1-58509-225-8 • 384 pages • 6 x trade paper • $28.95

The Divine Pymander: And Other Writings of Hermes Trismegistus, translated by John Chambers. ISBN 1-58509-046-8 • 196 pages • 6 x 9 • trade paper • $16.95

Theosophy and The Secret Doctrine, by Harriet L. Henderson. Includes ***H.P. Blavatsky: Outline of Her Life,*** by Herbert Whyte, ISBN 1-58509-075-1 • 132 pages • 6 x 9 • trade pape $13.95

The Light of Egypt, Volume One: The Science of the Soul and the Stars, by Thomas Burgoyne. ISBN 1-58509-051-4 • 320 pages • 6 x 9 • trade paper • illustrated • $24.95

The Light of Egypt, Volume Two: The Science of the Soul and the Stars, by Thomas Burgoyne. ISBN 1-58509-052-2 • 224 pages • 6 x 9 • trade paper • illustrated • $17.95

The Jumping Frog and 18 Other Stories: 19 Unforgettable Mark Twain Stories, by Ma Twain. ISBN 1-58509-200-2 • 128 pages • 6 x 9 • trade paper • $12.95

The Devil's Dictionary: A Guidebook for Cynics, by Ambrose Bierce. ISBN 1-58509-016- 144 pages • 6 x 9 • trade paper • $12.95

The Smoky God: Or The Voyage to the Inner World, by Willis George Emerson. ISBN 58509-067-0 • 184 pages • 6 x 9 • trade paper • illustrated • $15.95

A Short History of the World, by H.G. Wells. ISBN 1-58509-211-8 • 320 pages • 6 x 9 • tra paper • $24.95

The Voyages and Discoveries of the Companions of Columbus, by Washington Irving. ISBN 58509-500-1 • 352 pages • 6 x 9 • hard cover • $39.95

History of Baalbek, by Michel Alouf. ISBN 1-58509-063-8 • 196 pages • 5 x 8 • trade pape illustrated • $15.95

Ancient Egyptian Masonry: The Building Craft, by Sommers Clarke and R. Engelback. ISI 1-58509-059-X • 350 pages • 6 x 9 • trade paper • illustrated • $26.95

That Old Time Religion: The Story of Religious Foundations, by Jordan Maxwell and P Tice. ISBN 1-58509-100-6 • 103 pages • 6 x 9 • trade paper • $12.95

Jumpin' Jehovah: Exposing the Atrocities of the Old Testament God, by Paul Tice. ISBN 58509-102-2 • 104 pages • 6 x 9 • trade paper • $12.95

The Book of Enoch: A Work of Visionary Revelation and Prophecy, Revealing Div Secrets and Fantastic Information about Creation, Salvation, Heaven and Hell, translated R. H. Charles. ISBN 1-58509-019-0 • 152 pages • 5 1/2 x 8 1/2 • trade paper • $13.95

The Book of Enoch: Translated from the Editor's Ethiopic Text and Edited with an Enlarg Introduction, Notes and Indexes, Together with a Reprint of the Greek Fragments, edi by R. H. Charles. ISBN 1-58509-080-8 • 448 pages • 6 x 9 • trade paper • $34.95

The Book of the Secrets of Enoch, translated from the Slavonic by W. R. Morfill. Edited, w Introduction and Notes by R. H. Charles. ISBN 1-58509-020-4 • 148 pages • 5 1/2 x 8 1/2 • tr paper • $13.95

'f Heaven and Earth: Essays Presented at the First Sitchin Studies 'ay, edited by Zecharia Sitchin. Zecharia Sitchin's previous books ave sold millions around the world. This book, first published in 996, contains further information on his incredible theories about the rigins of mankind and the intervention by intelligences beyond the arth. Sitchin, in previous works, offers the most scholarly and con-incing approach to the ancient astronaut theory you will most cer-inly ever find. This book offers the complete transcript of the first itchin Studies Day, held in Denver, Colorado on Oct. 6, 1996. echaria Sitchin's keynote address opens the book, followed by six ther prominent speakers whose work has been influenced by Sitchin. he other contributors to the book include two university professors, clergyman, a UFO expert, a philosopher, and a novelist—who joined echaria Sitchin in Denver, Colorado, to describe how his findings nd conclusions have affected what they teach and preach. They all seem to agree that the yths of ancient peoples were actual events as opposed to being figments of imagina-ons. Another point of agreement is in Sitchin's work being the early part of a new para-igm—one that is already beginning to shake the very foundations of religion, archaeol-gy and our society in general. **BT-175 • ISBN 1-885395-17-5 • 164 pages • 5 1/2 x 8 1/2 trade paper • illustrated • $14.95**

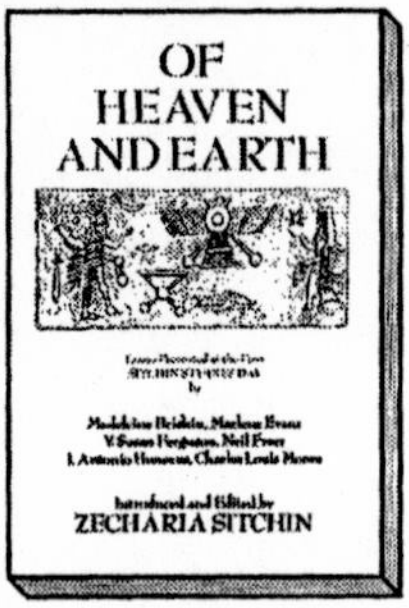

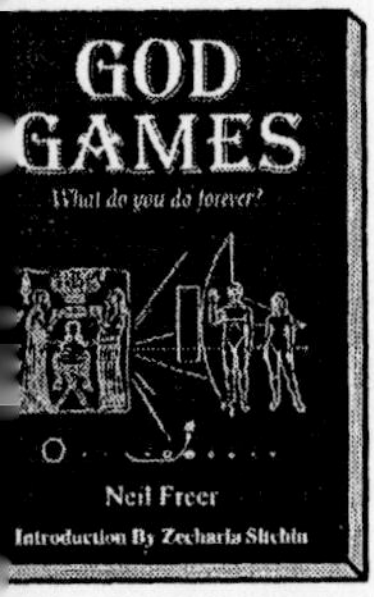

God Games: What Do You Do Forever? by Neil Freer. "Then came Neil Freer [who] undertook a different kind of mind-boggling task. If all that I had concluded was true, he said, what does it all mean, not to the human race and the planet in general—what does it mean to the individuals, to each one of us? He titles his new book *God Games*. But, if all the above is the Truth, it is not a game." Zecharia Sitchin (from the Introduction). This new book by Neil Freer, author of *Breaking the Godspell*, outlines the human evolutionary scenario far into the future. Freer describes what's in store for us as our dawning genetic enlightenment reveals the new human and the racial maturity of a new planetary civilization on the horizon. We all can contribute to our future as we evolve from a slave species to far beyond what we could previously even imagine. The godspell broken, we new humans 'ill create our own realities and play our own "god games." According to Freer, once we nderstand our true genetic history we will eventually move beyond the gods, religion, near consciousness and even death. It is quite possible that great thinkers in the future 'ill look back on this book as being the one which opened the door to our full evolu-onary potential and a new paradigm. Neil Freer is a brilliant philosopher, focused on the eedom of the individual and what it means to be truly human. This book will make you iink in new and different ways. Accept the challenge of *God Games* and you will be reatly rewarded. See page 16 for other products by Neil Freer. **BT-396 • ISBN 1-885395-9-6 • 312 pages • 6 x 9 • trade paper • $19.95**

'REAKING THE GODSPELL: THE POLITICS OF OUR 'VOLUTION, by Neil Freer. In *Breaking the Godspell* Neil Freer xplores the archaeological, astronomical and genetic evidence for ur being a half-alien, genetically engineered species. He presents the iind-boggling ramifications of this new paradigm which correct and :solve the Creationist-Evolutionary conflict, afford a generic defini-on of human nature, and the potential to rethink the planet. We are bout to step out of racial adolescence into stellar society. Zecharia itchin, author of *The 12th Planet* writes "It is gratifying that a mere ecade after the publication of my work, an author with the grasp that 'eil Freer displays in *Breaking the Godspell* has set out to probe what ie recognition of the existence and Earth-visits of the Nefilim can iean—not just to scientists and theologians—but to each human eing upon this planet Earth." This book is an encyclopedia of innovative ideas and ngaging speculation. It will alter your consciousness. It could change your life. BT-361 ISBN 1-885395-36-1 • 151 pages • 6 x 9 • trade paper • $15.95

Printed in the United Kingdom
by Lightning Source UK Ltd.
119743UK00001B/196